D0346950

Managing health and safety in construction

Construction (Design and Management) Regulations 2007

Approved Code of Practice

HSE Books

© Crown copyright 2007
First published 2007
ISBN 978 0 7176 6223 4

All rights reserved. No part of this publication may be
reproduced, stored in a retrieval system, or transmitted
in any form or by any means (electronic, mechanical,
photocopying, recording or otherwise) without the prior
written permission of the copyright owner.

Applications for reproduction should be made in writing to:
Information Policy Division, Her Majesty's Stationery Office,
The Office of Public Sector Information,
St Clements House, 2-16 Colegate, Norwich NR3 1BQ
Fax 01603 723000 or by e-mail to hmsolicensing@opsi.x.gsi.gov.uk

This Code has been approved by the Health and Safety Commission, with the
consent of the Secretary of State. It gives practical advice on how to comply with
the law. If you follow the advice you will be doing enough to comply with the law
in respect of those specific matters on which the Code gives advice. You may use
alternative methods to those set out in the Code in order to comply with the law.

However, the Code has a special legal status. If you are prosecuted for breach of
health and safety law, and it is proved that you did not follow the relevant
provisions of the Code, you will need to show that you have complied with the
law in some other way or a Court will find you at fault.

SHREWSBURY COLLEGE LIBRARY
INV. No. M1150733   DATE 28-1-08
ORD. No. 27720   DATE 052428 22-1-08
ACC. No.
15.40 CHECKED

Contents

Notice of approval

By virtue of Section 16(1) of the Health and Safety at Work etc. Act 1974, and with the consent of the Secretary of State for Work and Pensions, the Health and Safety Commission has on 13 February 2007 approved the Code of Practice entitled *Managing health and safety in construction*. The Code of Practice gives practical guidance with respect to the Construction (Design and Management) Regulations 2007, and comes into effect on 6 April 2007.

The revised Code of Practice under the Construction (Design and Management) Regulations 1994, which came into force on 4 September 2001, is hereby replaced with effect from 6 April 2007.

A reference in this Code of Practice to another document does not imply approval by the Health and Safety Commission of that document except to the extent necessary to give effect to this Code of Practice.

Signed

NEAL STONE
Acting Secretary to the Health and Safety Commission
13 February 2007

Introduction

1   The Construction (Design and Management) Regulations 2007 (CDM2007) come into force on 6 April 2007. They replace the Construction (Design and Management) Regulations 1994 (CDM94) and the Construction (Health, Safety and Welfare) Regulations 1996 (CHSW). This Approved Code of Practice (ACOP) provides practical guidance on complying with the duties set out in the Regulations. It replaces the ACOP to the Construction (Design and Management) Regulations 1994 from 6 April 2007.

2   The key aim of CDM2007 is to integrate health and safety into the management of the project and to encourage everyone involved to work together to:

(a)   improve the planning and management of projects from the very start;

(b)   identify hazards early on, so they can be eliminated or reduced at the design or planning stage and the remaining risks can be properly managed;

(c)   target effort where it can do the most good in terms of health and safety; and

(d)   discourage unnecessary bureaucracy.

3   These Regulations are intended to focus attention on planning and management throughout construction projects, from design concept onwards. The aim is for health and safety considerations to be treated as an essential, but normal part of a project's development – not an afterthought or bolt-on extra.

4   **The effort devoted to planning and managing health and safety should be in proportion to the risks and complexity associated with the project. When deciding what you need to do to comply with these Regulations, your focus should always be on action necessary to reduce and manage risks. Any paperwork produced should help with communication and risk management. Paperwork which adds little to the management of risk is a waste of effort, and can be a dangerous distraction from the real business of risk reduction and management.**

5   Time and thought invested at the start of the project will pay dividends not only in improved health and safety, but also in:

(a)   reductions in the overall cost of ownership, because the structure is designed for safe and easy maintenance and cleaning work, and because key information is available in the health and safety file;

(b)   reduced delays;

(c)   more reliable costings and completion dates;

(d)   improved communication and co-operation between key parties; and

(e)   improved quality of the finished product.

Typical operating and owning costs of a building* are in the ratio:

- 1 for construction costs;
- 5 for maintenance and building operating costs;
- 200 for business operating costs.

*Report of the Royal Academy of Engineering on *The long term costs of owning and using buildings* (1998)

Application of the Regulations

6 The Regulations are divided into five parts. Part 1 of the Regulations deals with matters of interpretation and application. The Regulations apply to all construction work in Great Britain and, by virtue of the Health and Safety at Work etc Act 1974 (Application outside Great Britain) Order 2001, its territorial sea, and apply to both employers and the self-employed without distinction.

7 Part 2 covers general management duties which apply to all construction projects, including those which are non-notifiable.

8 Part 3 sets out additional management duties which apply to projects above the notification threshold (projects lasting more than 30 days, or involving more than 500 person days of construction work). These additional duties require particular appointments or particular documents which will assist with the management of health and safety from concept to completion.

9 Part 4 of the Regulations applies to all construction work carried out on construction sites, and covers physical safeguards which need to be provided to prevent danger. Duties to achieve these standards are held by contractors who actually carry out the work, irrespective of whether they are employers or are self-employed. Duties are also held by those who do not do construction work themselves, but control the way in which the work is done. In each case, the extent of the duty is in proportion to the degree of control which the individual or organisation has over the work in question.

10 This does not mean everyone involved with design, planning or management of the project legally must ensure that all of the specific requirements in this section are complied with. They only have such duties if, in practice, they exercise significant control over the actual working methods, safeguards and site conditions. For example, contractors carrying out excavation work are normally responsible for ensuring that the excavation is safe to work at, but if a client specifies that it is dug and supported in a particular way, then the client will have a duty to ensure their instructions comply with the requirements in regulation 31.

11 Contractors must not allow work to start or continue unless the necessary safeguards are in place. For example, a brickwork contractor should not cause or permit workers under his control to work on an incomplete scaffold, even if providing the scaffold is another contractor's responsibility.

Regulations 3 and 25

12 Part 5 of the Regulations covers issues of civil liability; transitional provisions which will apply during the period when the Regulations come into force, and amendments and revocations of other legislation.

Definitions

Construction work

13 Construction work is defined in the Regulations. The following are not construction work as defined:

(a) putting up and taking down marquees and similar tents designed to be re-erected at various locations;

(b) general maintenance of fixed plant, except when this is done as part of other construction work, or it involves substantial dismantling or alteration of fixed plant which is large enough to be a structure in its own right, for

Regulation 2

ACOP

example structural alteration of a large silo; complex chemical plant; power station generator or large boiler;

(c) tree planting and general horticultural work;

(d) positioning and removal of lightweight movable partitions, such as those used to divide open-plan offices or to create exhibition stands and displays;

(e) surveying – this includes taking levels, making measurements and examining a structure for faults;

(f) work to or on vessels such as ships and mobile offshore installations;

(g) off-site manufacture of items for later use in construction work (for example roof trusses, pre-cast concrete panels, bathroom pods and similar pre-fabricated elements and components);

(h) fabrication of elements which will form parts of offshore installations;

(i) the construction of fixed offshore oil and gas installations at the place where they will be used.

14 Some construction projects include operations, such as those described in the previous paragraph, which are not themselves construction work. Where this is the case, the overlap between the construction and non-construction work should be addressed in the management arrangements and the construction phase plan.

Regulation 2

ACOP

Notification

15 Except where the project is for a domestic client, HSE must be notified of projects where construction work is expected to:

(a) last more than 30 working days; or

(b) involve more than 500 person days, for example 50 people working for over 10 days.

16 All days on which construction work takes place count towards the period of construction work. Holidays and weekends do not count if no construction work takes place on these days.

17 Where a small project that is not notifiable requires a short extension, or short-term increase in the number of people, there is no need to notify HSE. However, if the work or the scope changes significantly so that it becomes notifiable, HSE should be informed.

18 The information that has to be sent to HSE is set out in Schedule 1 to CDM2007. A form, F10(rev), can be used and is available from HSE's local offices (at www.hse.gov.uk/forms/notification/f10hseoffices.htm) or can be completed online (at www.hse.gov.uk/forms/notification/f10.pdf). You do not have to use this form, as long as you provide all of the specified information. Notification should be sent to the HSE offices that covers the site where the construction work is to take place (you can get addresses of HSE's local office from HSE's Infoline (see 'References' for details).

Regulations 2(3) and 21

19 CDM co-ordinators should notify HSE as soon as possible after their appointment. If the principal contractor is not appointed at that time then another,

ACOP

Regulations 2(3) and 21

updated, notification must be made after they have been appointed. Any missing information must be notified once it becomes available, and the notifier should make clear that it relates to an earlier notification. If a significant change occurs, it is helpful to notify HSE, for example when a new principal contractor is appointed or if the start date changes by a month or more.

ACOP

Co-operation and co-ordination

20   Although there is no requirement for the formal appointment of a CDM co-ordinator or principal contractor and for a construction phase plan for non-notifiable projects, regulations 5 and 6 do require co-operation and co-ordination between all members of the project team. For low risk projects, a low-key approach will be sufficient. In higher risk projects, for example those involving demolition, a more rigorous approach to co-ordination, co-operation and planning will be needed. Guidance given to CDM co-ordinators and principal contractors in this document gives an indication as to what is needed, but any action taken should be in proportion to the risk which the work creates. The architect, lead designer or contractor who is carrying out the bulk of the design work should normally co-ordinate the health and safety aspects of the design work; the builder or main contractor, if there is one, should normally co-ordinate construction work.

21   It is vital that those doing the work understand the risks involved and what to do about them. If the risks are low and the precautions well understood by those carrying out the work, then there will be no need for a written plan. In other simple cases a brief summary that clearly sets out who does what and in what order will be enough. Where the risks are higher, for example where the work involves:

(a)   structural alterations;

(b)   deep excavations, and those in unstable or contaminated ground;

(c)   unusual working methods or safeguards;

(d)   ionising radiation or other significant health hazards;

(e)   nearby high voltage powerlines;

(f)   a risk of falling into water which is, or may become, fast flowing;

(g)   diving;

(h)   explosives;

(i)   heavy or complex lifting operations;

then something closer to the construction phase plan will be needed. When carrying out demolition, regulation 29 requires those in control of the work to produce a written plan showing how danger will be prevented.

Regulations 5 and 6

ACOP

Taking account of the general principles of prevention

22   When considering what precautions are necessary to control risks associated with a project, everyone who has a duty under these Regulations must take account of the general principles of prevention specified in Schedule 1 to the Management of Health and Safety at Work Regulations 1999 ('the Management

Regulation 7

ACOP

Regulations'). These general principles are listed in Appendix 7. Further guidance on the application of the general principles of prevention can be found in the Approved Code of Practice for the Management of Health and Safety at Work Regulations 1999.[1]

Summary of the duties under the Regulations

23   A summary of the duties and how they are applied is given in the following table and chart.

	All construction projects (Part 2 of the Regulations)	Additional duties for notifiable projects (Part 3 of the Regulations)
Clients (excluding domestic clients)	■ Check competence and resources of all appointees ■ Ensure there are suitable management arrangements for the project including welfare facilities ■ Allow sufficient time and resources for all stages ■ Provide pre-construction information to designers and contractors	■ Appoint CDM co-ordinator* ■ Appoint principal contractor* ■ Make sure that the construction phase does not start unless there are suitable: - welfare facilities, and - construction phase plan in place ■ Provide information relating to the health and safety file to the CDM co-ordinator ■ Retain and provide access to the health and safety file **(* There must be a CDM co-ordinator and principal contractor until the end of the construction phase)**
CDM co-ordinators		■ Advise and assist the client with his/her duties ■ Notify HSE ■ Co-ordinate health and safety aspects of design work and co-operate with others involved with the project ■ Facilitate good communication between client, designers and contractors ■ Liaise with principal contractor regarding ongoing design ■ Identify, collect and pass on pre-construction information ■ Prepare/update health and safety file
Designers	■ Eliminate hazards and reduce risks during design ■ Provide information about remaining risks	■ Check client is aware of duties and CDM co-ordinator has been appointed ■ Provide any information needed for the health and safety file

Regulation 7

5

	All construction projects (Part 2 of the Regulations)	Additional duties for notifiable projects (Part 3 of the Regulations)
Principal contractors		■ Plan, manage and monitor construction phase in liaison with contractor ■ Prepare, develop and implement a written plan and site rules. (Initial plan completed before the construction phase begins) ■ Give contractors relevant parts of the plan ■ Make sure suitable welfare facilities are provided from the start and maintained throughout the construction phase ■ Check competence of all appointees ■ Ensure all workers have site inductions and any further information and training needed for the work ■ Consult with the workers ■ Liaise with CDM co-ordinator regarding ongoing design ■ Secure the site
Contractors	■ Plan, manage and monitor own work and that of workers ■ Check competence of all their appointees and workers ■ Train own employees ■ Provide information to their workers ■ Comply with the specific requirements in Part 4 of the Regulations ■ Ensure there are adequate welfare facilities for their workers	■ Check client is aware of duties and a CDM co-ordinator has been appointed and HSE notified before starting work ■ Co-operate with principal contractor in planning and managing work, including reasonable directions and site rules ■ Provide details to the principal contractor of any contractor whom he engages in connection with carrying out the work ■ Provide any information needed for the health and safety file ■ Inform principal contractor of problems with the plan ■ Inform principal contractor of reportable accidents, diseases and dangerous occurrences
Everyone	■ Check own competence ■ Co-operate with others and co-ordinate work so as to ensure the health and safety of construction workers and others who may be affected by the work ■ Report obvious risks ■ Comply with requirements in Schedule 3 and Part 4 of the Regulations for any work under their control ■ Take account of and apply the general principles of prevention when carrying out duties	

ACOP

Clients

24   The client has one of the biggest influences over the way a project is run. They have substantial influence and contractual control and their decisions and approach determine:

(a)   the time, money and other resources available for projects;

(b)   who makes up the project team, their competence, when they are appointed and who does what;

(c)   whether the team is encouraged to co-operate and work together effectively;

(d)   whether the team has the information that it needs about the site and any existing structures;

(e)   the arrangements for managing and co-ordinating the work of the team.

25   Because of this, they are made accountable for the impact their approach has on the health and safety of those working on or affected by the project. However, the Regulations also recognise that many clients know little about construction health and safety, **so clients are not required or expected to plan or manage projects themselves. Nor do they have to develop substantial expertise in construction health and safety, unless this is central to their business. Clients must ensure that various things are done, but are not normally expected to do them themselves.**

26   In the case of notifiable projects, clients must appoint a competent CDM co-ordinator. Those clients without construction expertise should rely on the CDM co-ordinator's advice on how best to meet their duties, but the CDM co-ordinator will need the client's support and input to be able to carry out their work effectively. The client remains responsible for ensuring that client duties are met.

27   Clients can also, intentionally or unwittingly, take on additional responsibilities. If they specify materials or methods of working they may well become designers in relation to those specific matters. They will also legally be contractors if they directly manage or carry out construction work.

Regulation 7

ACOP

Who are clients?

28   A client is an organisation or individual for whom a construction project is carried out. Clients only have duties when the project is associated with a business or other undertaking (whether for profit or not). This can include for example, local authorities, school governors, insurance companies and project originators on Private Finance Initiative (PFI) projects. Domestic clients are a special case and do not have duties under CDM2007.

Domestic clients

29   Domestic clients are people who have work done on their own home or the home of a family member, that does not relate to a trade or business, whether for profit or not. It is the type of client that matters, not the type of property. Local authorities, housing associations, charities, landlords and other businesses may own domestic property, but they are not domestic clients. If the work is in connection with the furtherance of a business attached to domestic premises, such as a shop, the client is not a domestic client.

Regulation 2

ACOP

30 Sometimes groups who would otherwise be domestic clients form companies to administer construction work. A common example of this is a company formed by leaseholders of flats to undertake maintenance of the common parts of a structure. In such a case, the company is not a domestic client, and will have duties under the Regulations.

31 Domestic clients have no client duties under CDM2007, which means that there is no legal requirement for appointment of a CDM co-ordinator or principal contractor when such projects reach the notification threshold. Similarly, there is no need to notify HSE where projects for domestic clients reach the notification threshold. However, designers and contractors still have their normal duties as set out in Parts 2 and 4 of the Regulations, and domestic clients will have duties under Part 4 of the Regulations if they control the way in which construction work is carried out (see paragraph 9).

32 Designers and contractors working for domestic clients have to manage their own work and co-operate with and co-ordinate their work with others involved with the project so as to safeguard the health and safety of all involved in the project. The requirements in Schedules 2 and regulations 25-44 and other health and safety law still apply.

Insurance and warranty claims

33 An insurance company arranging for construction work to be carried out under the terms of an insurance policy is the client for the purposes of CDM2007. However, where the insured arranges the work and the insurance company reimburses them, the insured is the client. If the latter is a domestic client they attract no duties under CDM2007.

34 If the insurer specifies designers or contractors for certain aspects of the work, then the insurer is responsible for establishing that they are competent.

35 It is common, with insurance-related work, for agents to be appointed to act on behalf of either the insured or insurer. These agents resolve claims and may co-ordinate the remedial works. Such agents may legally be clients with all the relevant duties.

36 Where remedial work is carried out under a home warranty scheme, such as those provided by the National House Building Council (NHBC), it is the provider of the warranty, for example NHBC, who is the client for the purposes of CDM2007.

Developers

37 In some instances, domestic clients may buy a house or flat before the whole project is complete, for example where house builders develop a site with a view to selling a number of homes. In such cases the purchaser may have an interest in the property, but it is still the developer who arranges for the construction work to be done and they are legally the client.

38 Builder-developers are often both client and principal contractor, although they may appoint another contractor as principal contractor. They may also be a designer or CDM co-ordinator. They must comply with CDM2007 in all their roles.

Regulation 2

ACOP

PFI, PPP and similar forms of procurement

39   Project originators are legally the client at the start of the project, and should ensure that a CDM co-ordinator is appointed and HSE notified during the early design and specification phase. The project originator cannot wait until someone else, for example the Special Purpose Vehicle (SPV), takes over the client role.

40   The role and responsibilities of the client can transfer from one party to another as the project proceeds. This is normally the case when the SPV is appointed to carry out detailed specification and delivery of the project. Any such transfer should:

(a)   be clear to, and agreed by all those involved;

(b)   be clearly recorded;

(c)   provide the practical authority to discharge the client's duties.

If the project originator does not wish to remain a client in respect of the Regulations after the SPV has been appointed, they should make use of the election facility in regulation 8. Without such an election, the project originator may retain some client responsibilities.

If there is doubt

41   In some circumstances it may not be immediately obvious who is legally the client and there can sometimes be more than one client involved in a project. **To avoid confusion, this needs to be resolved by those involved at the earliest stage possible.** Take into account who:

(a)   ultimately decides what is to be constructed, where, when and by whom;

(b)   commissions the design and construction work (the employer in contract terminology);

(c)   initiates the work;

(d)   is at the head of the procurement chain;

(e)   engages the contractors.

42   If there is still doubt, then all of the possible clients can appoint one of them as the only client for the purposes of CDM2007 (see regulation 8). Someone will always be the client. It is in the interests of all possible contenders to identify who it is. If not they run the risk that all will be considered to carry the client's duties under the Regulations.

Regulation 2

ACOP

What clients must do for all projects

43   Clients must make sure that:

(a)   designers, contractors and other team members that they propose to engage are competent (or work under the supervision of a competent person), are adequately resourced and appointed early enough for the work they have to do. Guidance on assessing competence is given in paragraphs 193-240;

Regulations 4-10

ACOP

(b)   they allow sufficient time for each stage of the project, from concept onwards;

(c)   they co-operate with others concerned in the project as is necessary to allow other dutyholders to comply with their duties under the Regulations;

(d)   they co-ordinate their own work with others involved with the project in order to ensure the safety of those carrying out the construction work, and others who may be affected by it;

(e)   there are reasonable management arrangements in place throughout the project to ensure that the construction work can be carried out, so far as is reasonably practicable, safely and without risk to health. (This does not mean managing the work themselves, as few clients have the expertise and resources needed and it can cause confusion);

(f)   contractors have made arrangements for suitable welfare facilities to be provided from the start and throughout the construction phase;

(g)   any fixed workplaces (for example offices, shops, factories, schools) which are to be constructed will comply, in respect of their design and the materials used, with any requirements of the Workplace (Health, Safety and Welfare) Regulations 1992;[3]

(h)   relevant information likely to be needed by designers, contractors or others to plan and manage their work is passed to them in order to comply with regulation 10.

Regulations 4-10

ACOP

Co-operation, co-ordination, timeliness and resources (see also paragraphs 20 and 21)

44   Co-operation between parties and co-ordination of the work are key to the successful management of construction health and safety. Co-operation and co-ordination can only be meaningful if the relevant members of the project team have been appointed early enough to allow them to contribute to risk reduction. This is particularly important during the design stage when both clients and contractors should contribute to discussions on buildability, usability and maintainability of the finished structure. Clients should seek to appoint those who can assist with design considerations at the earliest opportunity so that they can make a full contribution to risk reduction during the planning stages.

45   Unrealistic deadlines and a failure to allocate sufficient funds are two of the largest contributors to poor control of risk on site. When engaging designers and contractors, and for notifiable projects appointing CDM co-ordinators and principal contractors, clients have to consider the resources (for example staff, equipment and, particularly, time) needed to plan and do the work properly. Any contractors who are being considered for appointment should be informed of the minimum time period allowed to them for planning and preparation before construction work begins on site. Contractors should be given sufficient time after their appointment to allow them to plan the work and mobilise the necessary equipment (for example welfare facilities) and staff to allow the work to proceed safely and without risk to health. This is particularly important where the project involves demolition work - contractors must be given sufficient time for the planning and safe execution of any demolition activities.

Regulations 5, 6 and 9

46   Clients should consult with appointees (including the principal contractor) to find out how much time they will need for planning and preparation before work

ACOP

Regulations 5, 6 and 9

is expected to start in order that both parties can agree a suitable time period. Similarly, CDM co-ordinators will need sufficient time after their appointment to carry out their duties under the Regulations. Clients must then inform their appointees how much time the client has allowed for planning and preparation before the work starts.

ACOP

Arranging design work

47   Clients must only employ designers who are competent to carry out their CDM duties. Further help with assessing competence of designers is given in paragraphs 193-240.

48   Clients often employ more than one designer, for example architects, civil, structural and services engineers. In such cases they all need to know who does what, and the timing of the appointments needs to enable the design work to be co-ordinated from an early stage. Nominating one designer as the 'lead designer' is often the best way to ensure co-ordination and co-operation during work which involves a number of designers. For notifiable sites, this 'lead designer' may be appointed as a CDM co-ordinator under regulation 14, but the CDM co-ordinator's duties are wider than just design co-ordination and suitable arrangements must be made to carry out all of the CDM co-ordinator's tasks.

Regulations 4, 5 and 6

ACOP

Management arrangements

49   Most clients, particularly those who only occasionally commission construction work, will not be experts in the construction process and for this reason they are not required to take an active role in managing the work. Clients are required to take reasonable steps to ensure that suitable management arrangements are in place throughout the life of the project so that the work can be carried out safely and without risk to health. The arrangements put in place should focus on the needs of the particular job and should be proportionate to the risks arising from the work.

50   The client will need to ensure that arrangements are in place to ensure that:

(a)   there is clarity as to the roles, functions and responsibilities of members of the project team;

(b)   those with duties under the Regulations have sufficient time and resource to comply with their duties;

(c)   there is good communication, co-ordination and co-operation between members of the project team (for example between designers and contractors);

(d)   designers are able to confirm that their designs (and any design changes) have taken account of the requirements of regulation 11 (Designers' duties), and that the different design elements will work together in a way which does not create risks to the health and safety of those constructing, using or maintaining the structure;

(e)   that the contractor is provided with the pre-construction information (see paragraphs 55-60);

Regulation 9

(f)   contractors are able to confirm that health and safety standards on site will be controlled and monitored, and welfare facilities will be provided by the contractor from the start of the construction phase through to handover and completion.

51 Most of these arrangements will be made by others in the project team, such as designers and contractors. Before they start work, a good way of checking is to ask the relevant members of the team to explain their arrangements, or to ask for examples of how they will manage these issues during the life of the project. When discussing roles and responsibilities, on simple projects all that may be needed is a simple list of who does what. The main duties of project team members are listed in the table in the introduction to this Approved Code of Practice.

52 Having made these initial checks before work begins, clients should, as necessary, review to ensure that the arrangements which have been made are maintained. For non-notifiable projects, only simple checks will be needed, for example:

(a) checking that there is adequate protection for the client's workers and/or members of the public;

(b) checking to make sure that adequate welfare facilities have been provided by the contractor;

(c) checking that there is good co-operation and communication between designers and contractors;

(d) asking for confirmation from the contractor that the arrangements that they agreed to make have been implemented.

53 **Most clients on non-notifiable projects should be able to carry out these checks for themselves.** If you need help, this should be available from the competent person you have appointed under regulation 7 of the Management of Health and Safety at Work Regulations 1999. Alternatively, you could seek advice from someone who has acted as a CDM co-ordinator for a notifiable project, but you are not required to appoint a CDM co-ordinator unless the project is notifiable.

54 **When deciding whether management arrangements are suitable and maintained throughout the project, clients will need to make a judgement, taking account of the nature of the project and the risks that the work will entail. If this judgement is reasonable, and clearly based on the evidence requested and provided, clients will not be criticised if the arrangements subsequently prove to be inadequate, or if the company who has made the arrangements fails to implement them properly without the client's knowledge.**

Providing the pre-construction information

Example 1

A client was aware that there were electrical and gas services passing under the site. He arranged for plans for these to be provided by the relevant utility suppliers, and confirmed the exact location of the services by carrying out on-site tests. This information was then provided to contractors who were asked to tender for the work so that they could take account of the presence of the services when bidding for the work.

ACOP

55   Clients must provide designers and contractors who may be bidding for the work (or who they intend to engage), with the project-specific health and safety information needed to identify hazards and risks associated with the design and construction work. (The pre-construction information).

56   The information should be provided as part of the early procurement process or tendering, and responses to the issues identified can be a real help when judging competence of those tendering for the work. It therefore needs to be identified, assembled and sent out in good time, so that those who need it when preparing to bid or when preparing for the work can decide what resources (including time) will be needed to enable design, planning and construction work to be organised and carried out properly. Where design work continues during the construction phase, the pre-construction information will need to be provided to designers before work starts on each new element of the design. Similarly, where contractors are appointed during the construction phase, each contractor (or those who are bidding for the work) must be provided with the pre-construction information in time for them to take this into account when preparing their bid, or preparing for work on the site.

57   Clients who already have a health and safety file from earlier work, or who have previously carried out surveys or assessments, including assessments and plans under the Control of Asbestos at Work Regulations 2002 or the Control of Asbestos Regulations 2006,[2] may already have all, or much of the information needed. However, where there are gaps in this information, the client should ensure that these are filled by commissioning surveys or by making other reasonable enquiries. It is not acceptable for clients to make general reference to hazards which might exist - for example that '.... there may be asbestos present in the building'. Clients should carry out the necessary surveys in advance and provide the necessary information to those who need it.

> # The right information for the right people at the right time

58   The pre-construction information provided should be sufficient to ensure that significant risks during the work can be anticipated and planned for. It should concentrate on those issues that designers and contractors could not reasonably be expected to anticipate or identify, and not on obvious hazards such as the likelihood that the project would involve work at height. Appendix 2 lists topics that should be considered when drawing up the pre-construction information.

Example 2

A row of single storey brick-built garages was to be demolished. The site was to be completely fenced off. The pre-construction information stated that there were no hazardous substances or services to the garages. It provided details of the access route to the garages and stated that in recent months children had been playing in the area.

The principal contractor and demolition contractor agreed that no other information was needed.

Regulation 10

ACOP

Regulation 10

59   The information needs to be in a form that is convenient, ie clear, concise and easily understood, but it can be included in other documents, for example the specification, providing the relevant health and safety issues are fully covered. Brief notes on 'as built' drawings are particularly useful, but should be checked in case significant alterations have been carried out. In the case of notifiable projects, CDM co-ordinators will normally advise the client as to what is needed and arrange for relevant information to be given to designers and contractors. Guidance for CDM co-ordinators is given in paragraphs 84-108.

60   Clients are also required to tell contractors who they engage to carry out construction work (including, where relevant, principal contractors) the minimum notice that they will be given before they are expected to start construction work. This is to ensure that contractors have sufficient time to plan and prepare – for example mobilise their workforce and equipment, and make arrangements for welfare facilities to be provided (see Example 5).

ACOP

Regulations 5, 6 and 9(1)(b)

Welfare arrangements

61   Clients do not have to provide welfare facilities for construction workers, but if there are particular constraints which make it difficult for facilities to be provided, the client should co-operate with contractors and assist them with their arrangements.

ACOP

Additional things clients must do for notifiable projects

62   For notifiable projects, in addition to the duties set out above, clients must:

(a)   appoint a CDM co-ordinator to advise and assist with their duties and to co-ordinate the arrangements for health and safety during the planning phase;

(b)   appoint a principal contractor to plan and manage the construction work – preferably early enough for them to work with the designer on issues relating to buildability, usability and maintainability;

(c)   ensure that the construction phase does not start until the principal contractor has prepared a suitable construction phase plan and made arrangements for suitable welfare facilities to be present from the start of the work;

(d)   make sure the health and safety file is prepared, reviewed, or updated ready for handover at the end of the construction work. This must then be kept available for any future construction work or to pass on to a new owner.

Regulations 14, 15, 16 and 17

63   **Getting the right people for these roles and making early appointments is particularly important for clients with little construction or health and safety expertise, as they will need to rely on the advice given by the CDM co-ordinator on matters relating to the competence of those who they intend to appoint, and the adequacy of the management arrangements made by appointees.** For notifiable projects, if a client does not make these appointments they become legally liable for the work that the CDM co-ordinator and principal contractor should do, as well as for not making the appointments.

Appointment of the CDM co-ordinator

> **Example 3**
>
> A designer specified tilt and turn windows to reduce risks during window cleaning. The client overruled this on the grounds of cost. The designer pointed out that the client was taking over his duties under regulation 11, and needed to address how the risk to window-cleaners could be minimised and how the duties under the Workplace (Health, Safety and Welfare) Regulations 1992 could be complied with.

64   For notifiable projects, the client must appoint a competent, adequately resourced CDM co-ordinator as soon as practicable after initial design work or other preparations for construction work have begun. Guidance on the assessment of competence of a CDM co-ordinator can be found in paragraphs 193-240.

> **Example 4**
>
> On a large contract for a bank, worth several million pounds, the CDM co-ordinator was appointed late and given less than 48 hours to prepare the information.
>
> This meant that there was insufficient time to properly consider the plan. Work was delayed because the contractor had no information about the underground services to be found on site. In addition the co-ordinator was not able to ensure that health and safety aspects of the design had been properly addressed.

65   The CDM co-ordinator provides clients with a key project advisor in respect of construction health and safety risk management matters. Their main purpose is to help clients to carry out their duties; to co-ordinate health and safety aspects of the design work and to prepare the health and safety file.

66   Early appointment is crucial for effective planning and establishing management arrangements from the start. The Regulations require the appointment to take place as soon as is practicable after initial design work or other preparation for construction work has begun. This allows the client to appraise their project needs and objectives, including the business case and any possible constraints on development to enable them to decide whether or not to proceed with the project before appointing the CDM co-ordinator. The CDM co-ordinator needs to be in a position to be able to co-ordinate design work and advise on the suitability and compatibility of designs, and therefore they should be appointed before significant detailed design work begins. Significant detailed design work includes preparation of the initial concept design and implementation of any strategic brief. As a scheme moves into the detailed design stage, it becomes more difficult to make fundamental changes that eliminate hazards and reduce risks associated with early design decisions.

67   Proper consideration of the health and safety implications of the design for those who build and maintain the structure will make a significant contribution to reducing its whole life cost, and will make delivery to time, cost and quality more likely.

68   The CDM co-ordinator can be an individual or a company. CDM co-ordinators can be appointed independently of any other role on the project team, or they may combine this work with another role, for example, project manager,

designer or principal contractor. Where the role is combined, it is crucial that the CDM co-ordinator has sufficient independence to carry out their tasks effectively. The tasks can be shared out, but when this happens it is important to make sure that all of the duties are discharged. On simple projects, one person should be able to provide all of the support that clients need, but a team approach will be more common for larger or more complicated projects because of the workload and skills required.

Appointment of the principal contractor

69   For notifiable projects, clients must appoint one competent, adequately resourced principal contractor to plan, manage and monitor the construction work. Guidance on assessing the competence of principal contractors is given in paragraphs 193-240.

70   The principal contractor can be an organisation or an individual, and is usually the main or managing contractor. A principal contractor's key duty is to co-ordinate and manage the construction phase to ensure the health and safety of everybody carrying out construction work, or who is affected by the work.

> **Example 5**
>
> A client recognised that welfare facilities were required from the beginning of the construction phase. This meant services had to be installed early.
>
> To ensure that services would be available from the start of the construction phase, arrangements were made with utility companies for enabling works to be done before the contractor arrived on site.
>
> This reduced the lead-time required before construction could begin.

71   The principal contractor must be appointed as soon as the client knows enough about the project to select a suitable contractor. Early appointment allows the principal contractor and other specialists, for example maintenance contractors and facilities management experts to make a substantial contribution to ensuring the buildability and maintainability of the structure under construction. This helps to eliminate and reduce risks to health and safety, and to avoid interruptions, delays and other problems, which can add significantly to the costs of a project.

72   Early appointment is essential for the principal contractor to have sufficient time to develop an adequate construction phase plan and to arrange for appropriate resources, including welfare facilities, to be available when work commences on site. (Ensuring that welfare facilities are provided when work starts on site is a specific duty of the principal contractor, but the client also has a duty to make sure that the principal contractor has done so.) Principal contractors should be told as part of the pre-construction information the minimum amount of time which they will be given for planning and preparation before the construction work is expected to start on site (regulation 10(2)(c)).

73   There can only be one principal contractor at any one time. To ensure continuity, clients should normally keep the same principal contractor for the whole project from site clearance and preparation to final completion. However, there may be exceptions, for example where:

(a)   preliminary works, for example involving demolition or site preparation work, where there is a substantial delay between site clearance and the start of new construction work;

ACOP

(b) separate projects for different clients, for example for a building shell and subsequent fitting-out work.

74 In these cases, any change in principal contractor should:

(a) be clear to, and agreed by all those involved, particularly in relation to the timing of the change;

(b) be clearly recorded;

Regulations 4 and 14

(c) provide the practical authority to enable the principal contractor to discharge his duties.

ACOP

Management arrangements

75 For notifiable projects, clients must appoint a competent CDM co-ordinator who will assist them with the assessment of the adequacy of the management arrangements made by others in the project team. **Having appointed a competent CDM co-ordinator, the client is entitled to rely on their advice when making these judgements.** Guidance for CDM co-ordinators is covered in paragraphs 84-108.

Regulation 9

ACOP

Before the construction phase begins

76 For notifiable projects, before construction work begins clients must check to ensure that suitable welfare facilities have been provided, and that the construction phase plan has been prepared by the principal contractor. With the help of the CDM co-ordinator, clients must ensure that the plan is project-specific and suitable. Guidance on the content of the construction phase plan is given in Appendix 3.

77 Once the construction phase has begun, neither clients nor CDM co-ordinators have a duty to check that the plan is updated; this is the responsibility of the principal contractor.

Regulation 16

ACOP

The health and safety file

78 For notifiable projects, the health and safety file ('the file') is a source of information that will help to reduce the risks and costs involved in future construction work, including cleaning, maintenance, alterations, refurbishment and demolition. Clients therefore need to ensure that the file is prepared and kept available for inspection in the event of such work. It is a key part of the information, which the client, or the client's successor, must pass on to anyone preparing or carrying out work to which CDM2007 applies.

79 As soon as a CDM co-ordinator is appointed, clients should discuss and agree a suitable, user-friendly format for the file and what type of information it should contain. At the end of the construction phase, normally at practical completion, the file must be finalised and given to the client by the CDM co-ordinator. In some cases, for example where there is partial occupation or phased handover of a project it may be needed earlier to inform other work. For this to happen, CDM co-ordinators need to make appropriate arrangements at the beginning of the project to collect and compile the information that is likely to be needed for the file as work progresses. There is further information about the file and its contents in paragraphs 256-268.

Regulation 17

ACOP

Completion and handover (all projects)

80   One of the most important stages in a project is when it nears completion and is handed over to the client. It is rare for all construction work to be completed before handover. Sometimes clients, in their eagerness to have things up and running, assume control when a great deal of construction work remains.

81   Risks to employees and others not engaged in construction work can increase substantially as they visit the site or spend more time there. The risks to the construction workers can also increase, due to the presence and work of others not directly engaged or experienced in construction work.

82   To minimise such risks, the management of this phase needs to be considered well in advance to address:

(a)   the nature, scope and duration of any finishing-off work;

(b)   how this work will be managed and by whom;

(c)   how the site will be split up, and access controlled, to safeguard construction workers as well as clients' employees and/or members of the public.

For simple projects these arrangements can be discussed and agreed between the various parties. In more complex situations, the arrangements should be recorded as part of the construction phase plan.

What clients don't have to do

83   Clients are not required or expected to:

(a)   plan or manage construction projects themselves; or

(b)   specify how work must be done, for example requiring a structure to be demolished by hand. Indeed they should not do so unless they have the expertise to assess the various options and risks involved. (They should, of course, point out particular risks that would inform this decision.)

(c)   provide welfare facilities for those carrying out construction work (though they should co-operate with the contractor to assist with his arrangements);

(d)   check designs to make sure that regulation 11 has been complied with;

(e)   visit the site (to supervise or check construction work standards);

(f)   employ third party assurance advisors to monitor health and safety standards on site (though there may be benefits to the client in doing so);

(g)   subscribe to third party competence assessment schemes (though there may be benefits from doing so).

Regulation 9

ACOP

Regulation 9

ACOP

Regulation 14

ACOP

Regulations 20
and 21

The CDM co-ordinator (notifiable projects only)

84   The role of CDM co-ordinator is to provide the client with a key project advisor in respect of construction health and safety risk management matters. They should assist and advise the client on appointment of competent contractors and the adequacy of management arrangements; ensure proper co-ordination of the health and safety aspects of the design process; facilitate good communication and co-operation between project team members and prepare the health and safety file.

85   Through early involvement with clients and designers, a CDM co-ordinator can make a significant contribution to reducing risks to workers during construction, and to contractors and end users who work on or in the structure after construction.

Appointing the CDM co-ordinator

86   Early appointment of the CDM co-ordinator is crucial for effective planning and establishing management arrangements from the start. The Regulations require the appointment to take place as soon as is practicable after initial design work or other preparation for construction work has begun. This allows the client to appraise their project needs and objectives, including the business case and any possible constraints on development to enable them to decide whether or not to proceed with the project before appointing the CDM co-ordinator. The CDM co-ordinator needs to be in a position to be able to co-ordinate the health and safety aspects of the design work and advise on the suitability and compatibility of designs, and therefore they should be appointed before significant detailed design work begins. Significant detailed design work includes preparation of the initial concept design and implementation of any strategic brief. As a scheme moves into the detailed design stage, it becomes more difficult to make fundamental changes that eliminate hazards and reduce risks associated with early design decisions.

87   Proper consideration of the health and safety implications of the design for those who build and maintain the structure will make a significant contribution to reducing its whole life cost, and will make delivery to time, cost and quality more likely.

88   The CDM co-ordinator can be an individual or a company. They can be appointed independently of any other role on the project team, or they may combine this work with another role, for example, project manager, designer or principal contractor. Where the role is combined, it is crucial that the CDM co-ordinator has sufficient independence to carry out their tasks effectively. The tasks can be shared out, but when this happens it is important to make sure that all of the duties are discharged. On simple projects one person should be able to provide all of the support that clients need, but a team approach will be more common for larger or more complicated projects because of the workload and skills required.

89   Paragraphs 193-240 contain advice on selecting a competent CDM co-ordinator.

What CDM co-ordinators should do

90   CDM co-ordinators must:

(a)   give suitable and sufficient advice and assistance to clients in order to help them to comply with their duties, in particular:

ACOP

(i)   the duty to appoint competent designers and contractors; and

(ii) the duty to ensure that adequate arrangements are in place for managing the project;

(b)   notify HSE about the project (see paragraphs 15-19);

(c)   co-ordinate design work, planning and other preparation for construction where relevant to health and safety;

(d)   identify and collect the pre-construction information and advise the client if surveys need to be commissioned to fill significant gaps;

(e)   promptly provide in a convenient form to those involved with the design of the structure; and to every contractor (including the principal contractor) who may be or has been appointed by the client, such parts of the pre-construction information which are relevant to each;

(f)   manage the flow of health and safety information between clients, designers and contractors;

(g)   advise the client on the suitability of the initial construction phase plan and the arrangements made to ensure that welfare facilities are on site from the start;

Regulations 20 and 21

(h)   produce or update a relevant, user friendly, health and safety file suitable for future use at the end of the construction phase.

ACOP

Advising the client on competency of designers and contractors

Example 6

The CDM co-ordinator noted that a design required the heads of in situ cast pile caps to be broken down by hand, causing the team considerable exposure to noise and hand-arm vibration.

He suggested that by slightly redesigning the reinforcing steelwork and fitting it with protective sleeving before the pour, it would be possible to use either a machine-mounted concrete crusher or a hydraulic burster instead of hand-held breakers.

This suggestion was agreed with the designer and adopted, resulting in considerable time savings as well as reducing the health risk.

Regulations 4 and 20

91   Clients are responsible for appointing competent and adequately resourced designers and contractors (including principal contractors). A competent CDM co-ordinator will have the knowledge and expertise to assist clients with these assessments. Further advice on assessing the competence of dutyholders can be found in paragraphs 193-240.

Managing information flow

ACOP

Regulations 10, 15 and 20

92   Co-operation and co-ordination can only be achieved if there is good communication between all parties involved in a particular aspect of a project. During planning stages the CDM co-ordinator needs to make sure that there are appropriate systems in place to encourage communication and the sharing of relevant information, and CDM co-ordinators should manage the flow of information between the team members. They may need to convene special meetings if they are not satisfied there is sufficient co-operation between designers or with other team members, or if adequate regard is not being given to health and safety. It is, however, better for these issues to be addressed in routine project meetings.

Providing information

ACOP

Regulations 10, 15 and 20

93   Clients must provide designers and contractors who may be bidding for the work (or who they intend to engage), with the project-specific health and safety information needed to identify hazards and risks associated with the design and construction work. (The pre-construction information). For notifiable projects, clients are required to provide this information to the CDM co-ordinator. The CDM co-ordinator should check the information to ensure that it is complete, advise the client if there are any significant gaps or defects, and ensure these are filled by commissioning surveys or by making other reasonable enquiries. The CDM co-ordinator should then provide designers or contractors who may be bidding for, or preparing to carry out construction work on site, with such parts of the pre-construction information that are relevant to each.

94   Guidance on the content of the pre-construction information and when it should be provided is given in paragraphs 55-60 and Appendix 2.

Advising the client on adequacy of management arrangements

ACOP

95   Clients must make sure that there are suitable (project-specific) arrangements for managing each project so that the work can be carried out safely and without risk to health. Most clients, particularly those who only occasionally commission construction work, will not be experts in the construction process. The Regulations do not require clients to take an active role in managing the work, but they do require clients to take reasonable steps to ensure that suitable management arrangements are in place throughout the life of the project.

96   The CDM co-ordinator should assist with the development of these arrangements, and should advise clients on whether or not the arrangements are adequate. They should assist the client with decisions about how much time a contractor will need to prepare before construction work begins. When advising and assisting the client, the following issues should be considered.

(a)   Is the client aware of their duties and do they understand what is expected of them?

(b)   Has the client prepared relevant information about the site in order to meet their duties under regulation 10?

(c)   Have the necessary appointments been made, and has the project been notified?

Regulations 9 and 20

(d)   Is there an established project team who meet regularly to discuss and co-ordinate activities in relation to the project?

ACOP

(e)   Are project team members clear about their roles and responsibilities?

(f)   Are there arrangements in place for co-ordinating design work and reviewing the design to ensure that the requirements in regulation 11 are being addressed?

(g)   Are there arrangements in place for dealing with late changes to the design, and for co-operating with contractors, so that problems are shared?

(h)   Has the principal contractor been given enough time to plan and prepare for the work, and mobilise for the start of the construction phase?

(i)   Has the principal contractor made arrangements for providing welfare facilities on site from the outset, and have they prepared a construction phase plan that addresses the main risks during the early stages of construction?

(j)   Are there suitable arrangements for developing the plan to cover risks that arise as the work progresses?

(k)   Has the format for the health and safety file been agreed, and are arrangements in place for collecting the information which it will contain?

(l)   Has the principal contractor put in place suitable arrangements for consulting with workers on site; for carrying out site induction and for ensuring that workers are adequately trained and supervised?

97   Not all of these questions will need answers at the start of the project, and the arrangements will need to evolve as the project develops. The key thing is to plan ahead so that arrangements are in place before the risks that need managing materialise on site.

Regulations 9 and 20

ACOP

Co-ordinating design work: Design reviews

98   The CDM co-ordinator's legal responsibility in respect of design work only extends to health and safety aspects of the design – checking that the requirements of regulation 11 have been addressed and that the different design elements work together without causing danger. This is best achieved through design reviews during which health and safety issues are addressed alongside practicality and cost in a wider review of the design's buildability, maintainability and usability.

99   When considering buildability, meetings should where possible include the contractor(s) so that difficulties associated with construction can be discussed and solutions agreed before the work begins. When discussing usability and maintainability, involving the client or those who will be responsible for operating the building or structure will mean that proper consideration can be given to the health and safety of those who will maintain and use the structure once it has been completed. Doing this during the design stage will result in significant cost savings for the client, as rectifying mistakes after the structure has been built is always expensive.

100 As part of design reviews, CDM co-ordinators need to ensure that the designers have identified a safe method for construction for unusual or complex designs, and that the designs include the information needed by other designers and contractors to allow them to work safely and without risk to health. This information needs to be clear and concise.

Regulation 20

101 The timing of the reviews also needs careful consideration. Design needs to be far enough on for people to have a clear view of what is in mind, but not so far on that it is too late to modify the proposals, if necessary. Design is an iterative process so it may need review at several different stages. The effort devoted to design review should be in proportion to the risks and complexity.

102 CDM co-ordinators who identify important health and safety issues that have not been addressed in the design must draw them to the attention of the designer.

The CDM co-ordinator and the construction phase

103 Design often continues throughout a project and CDM co-ordinators have a continuing role during the construction phase – ensuring that designers, including those engaged by a contractor and contractors who carry out design work themselves, co-operate with each other, and designs meet the requirements of the Regulations. Where design changes and decisions during the construction phase have significant health and safety implications, CDM co-ordinators should liaise with the principal contractor about any implications for the construction phase plan.

104 The design of temporary works, such as falsework, formwork and scaffolding, falls within the scope of CDM2007. CDM co-ordinators have to take reasonable steps to ensure co-operation between permanent and temporary works designers, in particular to ensure that arrangements are in place to ensure that designs are compatible and that the permanent works can support any loadings from temporary works.

> **Example 7**
>
> The CDM co-ordinator together with the principal contractor ensured that the mechanical and electrical contractor for a multi-storey office block discussed the location of the services with the pre-cast floor contractor. This allowed the services drawings to be completed in time for service voids to be pre-formed in the pre-cast floors during the manufacturing stage.
>
> Operatives avoided significant exposure to noise and vibration from extensive diamond drilling on site. It was also significantly quicker and cheaper.

105 CDM co-ordinators need to pay particular attention to late designs or late changes to designs. Examples would be revisions on architects' instructions, when clients require changes or when unforeseen problems are encountered on site. The CDM co-ordinator should make sure that there are arrangements in place to ensure that such changes do not result in significantly increased risks on site.

Health and safety file

106 CDM co-ordinators must prepare a suitable health and safety file, or update it – if one already exists. It is important that they discuss this with the client before work starts on site so that the format can be agreed, along with who should provide what information, when. This requires the co-operation of several dutyholders, so CDM co-ordinators need to make sure that designers and contractors know, early on, what they will have to provide.

107 Clients may need to provide incentives or include requirements in contracts to ensure that the information is given to the CDM co-ordinator immediately after relevant design or construction work is completed. At the end of a project the

ACOP

CDM co-ordinator should give the completed file to the client for safekeeping (paragraphs 256-268 provide more information on the health and safety file.)

What CDM co-ordinators don't have to do

108 CDM co-ordinators don't have to:

(a) approve the appointment of designers, principal contractors or contractors, although they normally advise clients about competence and resources;

(b) approve or check designs, although they have to be satisfied that the design process addresses the need to eliminate hazards and control risks;

(c) approve the principal contractor's construction phase plan, although they have to be able to advise clients on its adequacy at the start of construction;

(d) supervise the principal contractor's implementation of the construction phase plan - this is the responsibility of the principal contractor; or

(e) supervise or monitor construction work – this is the responsibility of the principal contractor.

Regulations 17 and 20

ACOP

Designers

109 Designers are in a unique position to reduce the risks that arise during construction work, and have a key role to play in CDM2007. Designs develop from initial concepts through to a detailed specification, often involving different teams and people at various stages. At each stage, designers from all disciplines can make a significant contribution by identifying and eliminating hazards, and reducing likely risks from hazards where elimination is not possible.

110 Designers' earliest decisions fundamentally affect the health and safety of construction work. These decisions influence later design choices, and considerable work may be required if it is necessary to unravel earlier decisions. It is therefore vital to address health and safety from the very start.

> Example 8
>
> On a major office development with a large central atrium, the electrical contractor highlighted an innovative product for the roof glazing that was unknown to the other team members, including the designers. This was a double glazed unit incorporating internal prismatic reflectors.
>
> It removed the problem of glare and the need for high-level roller blinds. It was virtually maintenance free, and led to significant savings over the life the building, and significantly reduced the need to work at height.

111 Designers' responsibilities extend beyond the construction phase of a project. They also need to consider the health and safety of those who will maintain, repair, clean, refurbish and eventually remove or demolish all or part of a structure as well as the health and safety of users of workplaces. For most designers, buildability considerations and ensuring that the structure can be easily maintained and repaired will be part of their normal work, and thinking about the health and safety of those who do this work should not be an onerous duty. Failure to address these issues adequately at the design stage will usually increase running costs, because clients will then be faced with more costly solutions when repairs and maintenance become necessary.

112 Where significant risks remain when they have done what they can, designers should provide information with the design to ensure that the CDM co-ordinator, other designers and contractors are aware of these risks and can take account of them (see paragraphs 131-134).

113 Designers also have duties under other legislation, including those parts of the Management of Health and Safety at Work Regulations 1999 which require risk assessment. Compliance with regulation 11 of CDM2007 (as set out in paragraphs 109-145) will usually be sufficient for designers to achieve compliance with regulations 3(1), (2) and (6) of the Management Regulations as they relate to the design of the structure.

Regulations 17 and 20

114 Advice on the selection of competent designers is given in paragraphs 193-240.

ACOP

Who are designers?

115 Designers are those who have a trade or a business which involves them in:

(a) preparing designs for construction work, including variations. This includes preparing drawings, design details, specifications, bills of quantities and the

Regulation 2

specification (or prohibition) of articles and substances, as well as all the related analysis, calculations, and preparatory work; or

(b)   arranging for their employees or other people under their control to prepare designs relating to a structure or part of a structure.

It does not matter whether the design is recorded (for example on paper or a computer) or not (for example it is only communicated orally).

116   Designers therefore include:

(a)   architects, civil and structural engineers, building surveyors, landscape architects, other consultants, manufacturers and design practices (of whatever discipline) contributing to, or having overall responsibility for, any part of the design, for example drainage engineers designing the drainage for a new development;

(b)   anyone who specifies or alters a design, or who specifies the use of a particular method of work or material, such as a design manager, quantity surveyor who insists on specific material or a client who stipulates a particular layout for a new building;

(c)   building service designers, engineering practices or others designing plant which forms part of the permanent structure (including lifts, heating, ventilation and electrical systems), for example a specialist provider of permanent fire extinguishing installations;

(d)   those purchasing materials where the choice has been left open, for example those purchasing building blocks and so deciding the weights that bricklayers must handle;

(e)   contractors carrying out design work as part of their contribution to a project, such as an engineering contractor providing design, procurement and construction management services;

(f)   temporary works engineers, including those designing auxiliary structures, such as formwork, falsework, façade retention schemes, scaffolding, and sheet piling;

(g)   interior designers, including shopfitters who also develop the design;

(h)   heritage organisations who specify how work is to be done in detail, for example providing detailed requirements to stabilise existing structures; and

(i)   those determining how buildings and structures are altered, for example during refurbishment, where this has the potential for partial or complete collapse.

117   Local authority or government officials may provide advice relating to designs and relevant statutory requirements, for example the Building Regulations 2000,[4] but this does not make them designers. This is because these are legal requirements where the designer has no choice in respect of compliance. Any such requirements should be treated as 'design constraints' in the usual way. However, if the statutory bodies require that particular features which are not statutory requirements are included or excluded (for example stipulating the use of hazardous substances for cleaning or the absence of edge protection on flat roofs), then they are designers and must ensure that they comply with these CDM Regulations.

ACOP

Regulation 2

118 Manufacturers supplying standardised products that can be used in any project are not designers under CDM2007, although they may have duties under supply legislation. The person who selects the product is a designer and must take account of health and safety issues arising from its use. If a product is purpose-made for a project, the person who prepares the specification is a designer under CDM2007, and so is the manufacturer who develops the detailed design.

ACOP

What designers should do for all projects

119 Designers should:

(a) make sure that they are competent and adequately resourced to address the health and safety issues likely to be involved in the design;

(b) check that clients are aware of their duties;

(c) When carrying out design work, avoid foreseeable risks to those involved in the construction and future use of the structure, and in doing so, they should eliminate hazards (so far as is reasonably practicable, taking account of other design considerations) and reduce risk associated with those hazards which remain;

(d) provide adequate information about any significant risks associated with the design;

(e) co-ordinate their work with that of others in order to improve the way in which risks are managed and controlled.

120 In carrying out these duties, designers need to consider the hazards and risks to those who:

(a) carry out construction work including demolition;

(b) clean any window or transparent or translucent wall, ceiling or roof in or on a structure or maintain the permanent fixtures and fittings;

Regulations 4, 5, 6, 11 and 18

(c) use a structure designed as a place of work;

(d) may be affected by such work, for example customers or the general public.

ACOP

When do these duties apply?

121 These duties apply whenever designs are prepared which may be used in construction work in Great Britain. This includes concept design, competitions, bids for grants, modifications of existing designs and relevant work carried out as part of feasibility studies. It does not matter whether or not planning permission or funds have been secured; the project is notifiable or high-risk; or the client is a domestic client.

Regulations 11 and 12

ACOP

Making clients aware of their responsibilities

Regulation 11(1)

122 Designers are often the first point of contact for a client, and CDM2007 requires them to check that clients are aware of their duties under the Regulations.

ACOP

Example 9

A designer considered the use of a water-based paint for the exterior of a metal spire on a tall building to reduce exposure to solvents.

She determined that the level of exposure to solvents from a solvent-based paint would be low, and the metalwork would require more frequent repainting with a water-based paint.

She therefore concluded that it was better to specify the solvent-based paint because of the high risk of frequent working at height.

123 The duty to inform is aimed at the designer who has the initial or main contact with the client. Other designers need take no action unless they have reason to suspect that clients are not aware of their duties.

Regulation 11(1)

ACOP

Preparing a design

124 Designers have to weigh many factors as they prepare their designs. Health and safety considerations have to be weighed alongside other considerations, including cost, fitness for purpose, aesthetics, buildability, maintainability and environmental impact. CDM2007 allows designers to take due account of other relevant design considerations. The Regulations do not prescribe design outcomes, but they do require designers to weigh the various factors and reach reasoned, professional decisions.

125 **Designers are required to avoid foreseeable risks 'so far as is reasonably practicable, taking due account of other relevant design considerations'. The greater the risk, the greater the weight that must be given to eliminating or reducing it.** Designers are not expected to consider or address risks which cannot be foreseen, and the Regulations do not require zero risk designs because this is simply impossible. However, designers must not produce designs that cannot be constructed, maintained, used or demolished in reasonable safety.

126 Designers should critically assess their design proposals at an early stage, and then throughout the design process, to ensure that health and safety issues are identified, integrated into the overall design process and addressed as they go along. It is pointless to complete the design first, then try to address the risks which the design has introduced. By then, all of the key decisions are likely to have been taken and no one will be willing to make any changes because of the time and cost involved.

127 The first thing that designers need to do is eliminate hazards (things with a potential to cause harm) from their designs so far as is reasonably practicable, taking account of other design considerations. Examples would be to design out things like fragile roofing materials or products; eliminating rooflights from areas where roof access is needed; positioning plant which needs regular maintenance at ground level so there is no need for work at height or providing permanent safe access for work at height. Eliminating hazards removes the associated risk, and is therefore the best option and should always be the first choice.

Regulation 11(3), (4) and (5)

Example 10

A designer specified the use of lifting attachments. Not only did this reduce work at height, but it was estimated by the steel erectors that they were saving at least one hour per day.

ACOP

128 It is not always reasonably practicable to eliminate hazards, and where this is the case consideration should be given to incorporating design solutions which reduce the overall risk to an acceptable level. This can be done by reducing the:

(a)   likelihood of harm (injury or adverse health effect);

(b)   potential severity of the harm;

(c)   number of people exposed to the harm; and

(d)   frequency or duration of exposure to harm.

129 The amount of effort put into eliminating hazards and reducing risks should depend on the degree of risk. There is little point in spending a lot of money, time and trouble on low risk issues. There is also little to be gained by detailed comparison of construction techniques that present similar risks, for example whether to specify a steel frame or concrete portal building. The focus should be on issues that are known to have the potential to cause significant harm, and where there are known solutions that reduce the risks to everyone exposed.

130 Designers also need to take account of other relevant health and safety requirements when carrying out design work. Where the structure will be used as a workplace, (for example factories, offices, schools, hospitals) they need to take account of the provisions of the Workplace (Health, Safety and Welfare) Regulations 1992 which relate to the design of, or materials used in the structure. This means taking account of risks directly related to the proposed use of the structure, including associated private roadways and pedestrian routes, and risks arising from the need to clean and maintain the permanent fixtures and fittings. For example, hospitals will need to be designed in a way which will accommodate the safe lifting and movement of patients; food preparation and serving areas will need non-slip floors.

Regulation 11(3), (4) and (5)

ACOP

Providing information

> **Example 11**
>
> During the construction of a multi-storey office block the design sequence required the stairways to be installed progressively, as the floors were completed. This provided much quicker and safer access for people and materials than ladders.

> **Example 12**
>
> A designer considered using augered piles for a scheme to be built on contaminated land. He recognised that workers could be exposed to a toxic hazard. As a raft foundation was not viable from an engineering viewpoint, driven piles were specified. However, if augered piles had been the only reasonably practicable solution, the designer would have needed to include the possibility of exposure to toxic substances in the pre-construction information.

Regulation 11(6)

ACOP

131 Designers must provide information that other project team members are likely to need to identify and manage the remaining risks. **This should be project specific, and concentrate on significant risks which may not be obvious to those who use the design**. For example, providing generic risk information about the prevention of falls is pointless, because competent contractors will already know what needs to be done, but if the design gives rise to a specific and unusual fall risk which may not be obvious to contractors, designers should provide information about this risk.

132 Designers also need to provide information about aspects of the design that could create significant risks during future construction work or maintenance. If in doubt about the level of information needed, the best way to find out is to ask those who will use it.

133 Significant risks are not necessarily those that involve the greatest risks, but those, including health risks that are:

(a) not likely to be obvious to a competent contractor or other designers;

(b) unusual; or

(c) likely to be difficult to manage effectively.

134 Information should be brief, clear, precise, and in a form suitable for the users. This can be achieved using:

(a) **notes on drawings** – this is preferred, since the notes will then be immediately available to those carrying out the work. They can refer to other documents if more detail is needed, and be annotated to keep them up to date;

(b) **written information provided with the design** - this should be project specific, and should only contain information which will be useful to those constructing or maintaining the structure;

(c) **suggested construction sequences** showing how the design could be erected safely, where this is not obvious, for example suggested sequences for putting up pre-cast panel concrete structures. Contractors may then adopt this method or develop their own approach.

It is not always possible to provide all the information at the same time, particularly when design work is continuing whilst construction work is underway. In these circumstances information should be released as the design develops, but construction work should not be allowed to proceed unless all the information necessary for the work to be carried out safely has been provided.

Regulation 11(6)

ACOP

Co-operation

Example 13

A structural engineering consultancy was engaged to provide detailed design drawings for the steelwork to be incorporated in a complex alteration to an existing structure. The company recognised that many of the structural steel elements were of different lengths and the site layout meant that it would be difficult to lift the beams into position during assembly. The structural engineer ensured that simple lifting brackets were designed into each structural steel element, and that the lifting points were marked on the design drawings. This reduced the likelihood of error on site and the time taken for installation of the steel was reduced by a third.

Regulation 5

135 Designers must co-operate with the client, and other designers and contractors, including those designing temporary works. This is to ensure that incompatibilities between designs are identified and resolved as early as possible, and that the right information is provided in the pre-construction information.

136 For smaller projects where most of the work is done by a single designer, this can be achieved through discussion with those who use or are affected by the design. For larger projects or those involving significant risks, a more managed approach will be necessary.

137 Co-operation can be encouraged by:

(a) setting up an integrated team involving designers, principal contractor and other relevant contractors;

(b) the appointment of a lead designer, where many designers are involved (see paragraph 48);

(c) agreeing a common approach to risk reduction during design;

(d) regular meetings of all the design team (including the CDM co-ordinator) with contractors, and others;

(e) regular reviews of developing designs;

(f) site visits, through which designers can gain a direct insight into how the risks are managed in practice.

138 Regular reviews of the design involving all members of the design team are particularly important in making sure that proper consideration is given to buildability, usability and maintainability. When considering buildability, meetings should include the contractor so that difficulties associated with construction can be discussed and solutions agreed before the work begins. When discussing usability and maintainability, involving the client or those who will be responsible for operating the building or structure will mean that proper consideration can be given to the health and safety of those who will maintain and use the structure once it has been completed. Doing this during the design stage will result in significant cost savings for the client, as rectifying mistakes after the structure has been built is always expensive.

Additional duties where the project is notifiable

139 In addition to the duties outlined above, when the project is notifiable, designers should:

(a) ensure that the client has appointed a CDM co-ordinator;

(b) ensure that they do not start design work other than initial design work unless a CDM co-ordinator has been appointed;

(c) co-operate with the CDM co-ordinator, principal contractor and with any other designers or contractors as necessary for each of them to comply with their duties. This includes providing any information needed for the pre-construction information or health and safety file.

140 For a notifiable project, designers need to ensure that a CDM co-ordinator has been appointed. If appointment has been done, then designers can assume that the client is aware of their duties.

ACOP

141 Early appointment of the CDM co-ordinator is crucial for effective planning and establishing management arrangements from the start. The Regulations require the appointment to take place as soon as is practicable after initial design work or other preparation for construction work has begun. Guidance on the timing of appointment of the CDM co-ordinator is given in paragraph 66.

142 Once the CDM co-ordinator has been appointed, the designer will need to co-operate with them and provide the information which the CDM co-ordinator needs to comply with their duties.

What designers don't have to do

143 Under CDM2007, designers don't have to:

(a) take into account or provide information about unforeseeable hazards and risks;

(b) design for possible future uses of structures that cannot reasonably be anticipated from their design brief;

(c) specify construction methods, except where the design assumes or requires a particular construction or erection sequence, or where a competent contractor might need such information;

(d) exercise any health and safety management function over contractors or others; or

(e) worry about trivial risks.

> ### Example 14
>
> An air conditioning system, which included a water cooling tower, was refurbished as part of a factory extension.
>
> The designer made sure that the system complied with current design standards and included safe access for cleaning and maintenance. Information was provided to the occupier on maintenance and testing of the system to ensure the control of legionella.

144 Designers are not legally required to keep records of the process through which they achieve a safe design, but it can be useful to record why certain key decisions were made. Brief records of the points considered, the conclusions reached, and the basis for those conclusions, can be very helpful when designs are passed from one designer to another. This will reduce the likelihood of important decisions being reversed by those who may not fully understand the implications of doing so.

145 Too much paperwork is as bad as too little, because the useless hides the necessary. Large volumes of paperwork listing generic hazards and risks, most of which are well known to contractors and others who use the design are positively harmful, and suggest a lack of competence on the part of the designer.

Regulation 5

ACOP

The principal contractor (notifiable projects only)

146 Good management of health and safety on site is crucial to the successful delivery of a construction project. The key duty of principal contractors is to properly plan, manage and co-ordinate work during the construction phase in order to ensure that the risks are properly controlled. Principal contractors must also comply with the duties placed on all contractors under the Regulations.

147 Principal contractors are usually the main or managing contractor. This allows the management of health and safety to be incorporated into the wider management of project delivery. This is good business practice as well as being helpful for health and safety purposes.

148 Although written plans are only legally required for notifiable projects, all projects must be properly planned and managed, and the principles set out in this section may be relevant to those who plan for non-notifiable projects.

Regulation 5

149 Advice on selection of a competent principal contractor is given in paragraphs 193-240.

ACOP

What principal contractors must do

150 Principal contractors must:

(a) satisfy themselves that clients are aware of their duties, that a CDM co-ordinator has been appointed and HSE notified before they start work;

(b) make sure that they are competent to address the health and safety issues likely to be involved in the management of the construction phase;

(c) ensure that the construction phase is properly planned, managed and monitored, with adequately resourced, competent site management appropriate to the risk and activity.

(d) ensure that every contractor who will work on the project is informed of the minimum amount of time which they will be allowed for planning and preparation before they begin work on site;

(e) ensure that all contractors are provided with the information about the project that they need to enable them to carry out their work safely and without risk to health. Requests from contractors for information should be met promptly;

(f) ensure safe working and co-ordination and co-operation between contractors;

(g) ensure that a suitable construction phase plan ('the plan') is:

   (i) prepared before construction work begins,

   (ii) developed in discussion with, and communicated to, contractors affected by it,

   (iii) implemented, and

Regulations 4, 5, 6 and 22-24 and Part 4 of the Regulations

   (iv) kept up to date as the project progresses;

ACOP

(h)	satisfy themselves that the designers and contractors that they engage are competent and adequately resourced (see paragraphs 193-240);

(i)	ensure suitable welfare facilities are provided from the start of the construction phase;

(j)	take reasonable steps to prevent unauthorised access to the site;

(k)	prepare and enforce any necessary site rules;

(l)	provide (copies of or access to) relevant parts of the plan and other information to contractors, including the self-employed, in time for them to plan their work;

(m)	liaise with the CDM co-ordinator on design carried out during the construction phase, including design by specialist contractors, and its implications for the plan;

(n)	provide the CDM co-ordinator promptly with any information relevant to the health and safety file (see paragraphs 256-268);

(o)	ensure that all the workers have been provided with suitable health and safety induction, information and training;

(p)	ensure that the workforce is consulted about health and safety matters (see paragraphs 241-255);

(q)	display the project notification.

Regulations 4, 5, 6 and 22-24 and Part 4 of the Regulations

ACOP

Co-operation and co-ordination

151	Good co-operation and co-ordination of work between all of the parties involved in a project is essential if risks are to be identified early on and properly controlled. Principal contractors should take the lead and actively encourage co-operation and co-ordination between contractors from an early stage. A team approach involving the client, designers, contractors and even manufacturers who work closely together will often produce the best results. This allows the client, designers, contractors and facilities management experts, together, to identify the best solution for the client's needs, taking account of the practicalities of construction work, maintenance and use. Even on projects where it is not practical to formally establish an integrated team, the client, designer, contractors and others involved in the project still need to work together.

152	If there are other projects on the same or neighbouring sites (for example adjacent units on the same industrial estate) then the co-operation and co-ordination needs to extend to those involved with such projects. If this need can be identified early on, the risks that one project may cause for the other can also be identified and addressed in the early stages of project planning. If potential problems are not identified until the actual work has started they can be much more difficult to address.

153	Good, timely communication is essential to co-operation and co-ordination of activities. Information about risks and precautions needs to be shared sensibly (ie relevant information, not everything) when it is needed to plan and manage work. Drawings can be used to highlight hazards or unusual work sequences identified by designers, with advice on where to find more information, if required. Induction training and toolbox talks help to ensure workers understand

Regulations 5 and 6

ACOP
Regulations 5 and 6

the risks and precautions, and are a good opportunity to inform workers of site rules or any special risks relating to the project.

How many principal contractors can there be for each project?

ACOP

154 There can only be one principal contractor for a project at any one time. However, sometimes two or more projects take place on a site at the same time. This can occur if different clients commission adjacent work, or if a client procures two truly independent, unrelated packages of work which do not rely upon one another for their viability or completion.

155 Where overlapping projects are running on a single construction site, it is best to appoint one principal contractor for them all. If this is not done, all the principal contractors must co-operate, and their plans must take account of the interfaces – for example in traffic management. The requirements of regulations 8, 9 and 11 of the Management Regulations are also relevant.

Regulation 14(2)

Planning and managing health and safety in the construction phase

ACOP

156 Principal contractors must plan, manage and co-ordinate work during the construction phase taking account of the information contained in the pre-construction information provided by the client, and any other information provided by contractors.

157 The effort devoted to planning and managing health and safety should be in proportion to the risks and complexity associated with the project.

158 The principal contractor should work with other contractors to identify the hazards and assess the risks related to their work, including the risks they may create for others. Using this information and applying the general principles of prevention (see Appendix 7) the principal contractor, in discussion with the contractors involved, must plan, manage and co-ordinate the construction phase. This includes supervising and monitoring work to ensure that it is done safely and that it is safe for new activities to begin.

159 Where the project involves high-risk work, for example alterations that could result in structural collapse, or work on contaminated land, specialist advice is likely to be needed at the planning stage.

Example 15

On a busy construction site employing several contractors, the key details of the construction phase plan were transferred to a wall chart and displayed in the site office and in the canteen. This enabled all visitors and workers on site to find relevant information quickly and easily. The chart was reviewed on a weekly basis and any necessary revisions made.

Regulation 22(1)(a)

The construction phase plan

ACOP

160 The way in which the construction phase will be managed and the key health and safety issues for the particular project must be set out in writing in the construction phase plan. This plan should set out the organisation and arrangements that have been put in place to manage risk and co-ordinate the work on site. It should not be a repository for detailed generic risk assessments, records of how decisions were reached or detailed method statements, but it may, for example set out when such documents will need to be prepared. It should be well

Regulation 23

focused, clear and easy for contractors and others to understand – emphasising key points and avoiding irrelevant material. It is crucial that all relevant parties are involved and co-operate in the development and implementation of the plan as work progresses.

161 **The plan must be tailored to the particular project.** Generic plans that do not contain the information relevant to the particular risks associated with the work will not satisfy the requirements of regulation 23. Photographs and sketches can greatly simplify and shorten explanations. It should also be organised so that relevant sections can easily be made available to designers and contractors.

162 Often the design and preparation for later work is not complete at the start of the construction phase. Nevertheless, the plan for the initial phase of the construction work must be prepared before any work begins. It should also address later activities that will require careful planning. It may only be practical to address such activities in outline form before work starts and most will require revision in the light of developments.

163 The topics that need to be addressed when developing the construction phase plan are shown at Appendix 3. Where other available documents address these issues appropriately, the plan may refer to them; the information does not need to be repeated.

Implementing and monitoring the plan

164 A plan is no use if it is treated as merely a paper exercise and gathers dust. To improve standards, it must be a practical aid to the management of health and safety on site. Principal contractors and other contractors have a particular role in both implementing and monitoring the plan to ensure that it works in practice. Monitoring arrangements will need to be discussed and agreed with the client as they form part of the management arrangements.

165 The purpose of monitoring is to ensure that the precautions described in the construction phase plan are appropriate and followed in practice. **Where contractors do not work safely or comply with the plan, principal contractors must take appropriate action to deal with the risk. (They can give reasonable directions to any contractor and contractors have to comply, whether they have been appointed by the principal contractor or not – regulation 19(2)).** Principal contractors are responsible for ensuring the health and safety of everyone on site. Everyone on site (including the client, anyone working for the client and workers of utility companies) must co-operate with the principal contractor to enable them to comply with their duties.

> Example 16
>
> New chemical processing plant was being installed in a factory. The clients had included requirements in relation to the safety of their workforce and plant in the pre-construction information. The information included details of those parts of the site the client would continue to occupy, information about the permit-to-work system, emergency procedures and traffic management arrangements. Regular meetings were held to ensure good communication and co-ordination.

166 The plan needs to be routinely reviewed, revised and refined by the principal contractor as the project develops. For example, where the plan is not being followed, and health and safety is put at risk, those involved must take appropriate action to deal with the risk. Monitoring may show the plan has

ACOP
Regulation 23

ACOP

shortcomings and needs to be modified. Any significant changes in the plan should be brought to the attention of all those affected.

Site rules

167 Principal contractors should include any necessary rules for the management of construction work in the construction phase plan, which others on the site have to follow. These may cover issues such as restricted areas, permit-to-work systems, hot work and emergency plans. In order to avoid cluttering the plan with detailed arrangements for implementing site rules, the plan should refer to other documents or put detailed arrangements in appendices. Site rules should be:

(a)   set out in writing;

(b)   understandable to those who have to follow them;

(c)   brought to the attention of everyone who has to follow them;

(d)   enforced.

Regulation 22(1)(d)

168 Copies of the site rules should be displayed on site in a place where they can be seen by those who work there.

ACOP

Regulation 22(1)(k)

Display of notification to HSE

169 The principal contractor must display a legible copy of the most up-to-date information notified to HSE where it can be read by people working on the site.

ACOP

Controlling access onto sites

170 A principal contractor must take reasonable steps to prevent access by unauthorised persons to the construction site. Only people who are explicitly authorised, individually or collectively, by the principal contractor, should be allowed access. The authorisation may cover the whole site or be restricted to certain areas. Authorised people should have relevant site rules explained to them and undertake any necessary site induction, and should comply with site rules and co-operate with the principal contractor. Some authorised visitors may need to be supervised or accompanied while on site or visiting specific areas.

171 How access is controlled depends on the nature of the project, the risks and location. The boundaries of all sites should be physically defined, where necessary, by suitable fencing. The type of fencing should reflect the nature of the site and its surroundings. Special consideration is needed where:

(a)   rights of way cross sites;

(b)   sites are in, or next to, other work areas;

(c)   new houses are being built on a development where some houses are already occupied; or

Regulation 22(1)(l)

(d)   there are children or other vulnerable people nearby.

ACOP

Example 17

A site compound was set up near the site entrance. This meant that every person who entered or left the site had to pass through the compound, where a register was kept listing all those who entered or left the site.

172 The effectiveness of the arrangements needs to be reviewed in the light of experience. In particular, their adequacy should be carefully reviewed if there is evidence of children playing on, or near the site.

Example 18

In addition to a site-specific safety induction, every worker who entered the site was provided with a small pocket card detailing the site health and safety rules. Any new rules introduced as a result of work being carried out on the site were clearly displayed at the site entrance and the cards were reprinted and re-issued.

Regulation 22(1)(l)

ACOP

Site induction, training and information

173 Site induction, training and information are vital to securing health and safety on site. The principal contractor has to ensure, so far as is reasonably practicable, that every worker has:

(a)   a suitable induction; and

(b)   any further information and training needed for the particular work.

This does not mean that the principal contractor has to train everyone on the site - this will be the responsibility of individual contractors. Further advice on training and competence is given in paragraphs 193-240.

Induction

174 Inductions are a way of providing workers with specific information about the particular risks associated with the site and the arrangements that have been made for their control. Induction is not intended to provide general health and safety training, but it should include a site-specific explanation of the following:

(a)   senior management commitment to health and safety;

(b)   the outline of the project;

(c)   the individual's immediate line manager and any other key personnel;

(d)   any site-specific health and safety risks, for example in relation to access, transport, site contamination, hazardous substances and manual handling;

(e)   control measures on the site, including:

(i)   any site rules,

(ii)   any permit-to-work systems,

Regulation 22(2)

(iii) traffic routes,

ACOP

(iv)   security arrangements,

(v)   hearing protection zones,

(vi)   arrangements for personal protective equipment, including what is needed, where to find it and how to use it,

(vii) arrangements for housekeeping and materials storage,

(viii) facilities available, including welfare facilities,

(ix)   emergency procedures, including fire precautions, the action to take in the event of a fire, escape routes, assembly points, responsible people and the safe use of any fire-fighting equipment;

(f)   arrangements for first aid;

(g)   arrangements for reporting accidents and other incidents;

(h)   details of any planned training, such as 'toolbox' talks;

(i)   arrangements for consulting and involving workers in health and safety, including the identity and role of any:

(i)   appointed trade union safety representatives,

(ii)   representatives of employee safety,

(iii) safety committees;

(j)   information about the individual's responsibilities for health and safety.

> **Example 19**
>
> All new employees on a large transport infrastructure project attended an induction session, in works time, on their first day. Employer and trade union representatives jointly explained the key issues.
>
> The joint approach reinforced the messages and made the induction more effective.

What principal contractors don't have to do

Regulation 22(2)

175 Principal contractors don't have to undertake detailed supervision of contractors' work.

ACOP

Contractors and the self-employed

176 Contractors and those actually doing the construction work are most at risk of injury and ill health. They have a key role to play, in co-operation with the principal contractor, in planning and managing the work to ensure that risks are properly controlled.

177 All contractors (including utilities, specialist contractors, contractors nominated by the client and the self-employed) have a part to play in ensuring that the site is a safe and healthy place to work. The key to this is the proper co-ordination of the work, underpinned by good communication and co-operation between all those involved.

178 Anyone who directly employs, engages construction workers or controls or manages construction work is a contractor for the purposes of these Regulations. This includes companies that use their own workforce to do construction work on their own premises. The duties on contractors apply whether the workers are employees or self-employed and to agency workers without distinction.

Regulation 22(2)

ACOP

What contractors must do on all projects

179 For all projects contractors must:

(a) check clients are aware of their duties;

(b) satisfy themselves that they and anyone they employ or engage are competent and adequately resourced;

(c) plan, manage and monitor their own work to make sure that workers under their control are safe from the start of their work on site;

(d) ensure that any contractor who they appoint or engage to work on the project is informed of the minimum amount of time which will be allowed for them to plan and prepare before starting work on site;

(e) provide workers under their control (whether employed or self-employed) with any necessary information, including about relevant aspects of other contractors' work, and site induction (where not provided by a principal contractor) which they need to work safely, to report problems or to respond appropriately in an emergency;

(f) ensure that any design work they do complies with regulation 11;

(g) comply with any requirements listed in Schedule 2 and Part 4 of these Regulations that apply to their work;

(h) co-operate with others and co-ordinate their work with others working on the project;

(i) ensure the workforce is properly consulted on matters affecting their health and safety; and

(j) obtain specialist advice (for example from a structural engineer or occupational hygienist) where necessary when planning high-risk work – for example alterations that could result in structural collapse or work on contaminated land.

Regulations 4-6, 13 and Part 4

ACOP

Regulation 13(2)

Planning and managing construction work

180 Contractors should always plan, manage, supervise and monitor their own work and that of their workers to ensure that it is carried out safely and that health risks are also addressed. The effort invested in this should reflect the risk involved and the experience and track record of the workers involved. Where contractors identify unsafe practices, they must take appropriate action to ensure health and safety.

181 If one contractor is overseeing the work for a domestic client then they should ensure that the work of the various contractors is properly co-ordinated, and that there is good co-operation and communication (see paragraphs 20 and 21).

ACOP

Regulation 13(4)

Site induction, information and training

182 Contractors must not start work on a construction site until they have been provided with basic information. This should include information from the client about any particular risks associated with the project (including information about existing structures where these are to be demolished or structurally altered), and from designers about any significant risks associated with the design.

183 Contractors must ensure, so far as is reasonably practicable, that every worker has:

(a) a suitable induction; and

(b) any further information and training needed for the particular work.

Further advice on training and competence is given in paragraphs 193-240.

ACOP

Regulation 13(4)(a)

Induction (see Example 19)

184 Inductions are a way of providing workers with specific information about the particular risks associated with the site and the arrangements which have been put in place for their control. On non-notifiable sites, induction will need to be provided by the contractor, or by arrangement with the main contractor on site.

185 Induction is not intended to provide general health and safety training, but it should include a site-specific explanation of the following:

(a) senior management commitment to health and safety;

(b) the outline of the project;

(c) the individual's immediate line manager and any other key personnel;

(d) any site-specific health and safety risks, for example in relation to access, transport, site contamination, hazardous substances and manual handling;

(e) control measures on the site, including:

    (i) any site rules,

    (ii) any permit-to-work systems,

    (iii) traffic routes,

ACOP

    (iv)   security arrangements,

    (v)   hearing protection zones,

    (vi)   arrangements for personal protective equipment, including what is needed, where to find it and how to use it,

    (vii)   arrangements for housekeeping and materials storage,

    (viii) facilities available, including welfare facilities,

    (ix)   emergency procedures, including fire precautions, the action to take in the event of a fire, escape routes, assembly points, responsible people and the safe use of any fire-fighting equipment;

(f)   arrangements for first aid;

(g)   arrangements for reporting accidents and other incidents;

(h)   details of any planned training, such as 'toolbox' talks;

(i)   arrangements for consulting and involving workers in health and safety, including the identity and role of any:

    (i)   appointed trade union representatives,

    (ii)   representatives of employee safety,

    (iii)   safety committees;

Regulation 13(4)(a)

(j)   information about the individual's responsibilities for health and safety.

ACOP

Reporting incidents

186 The Reporting of Injuries, Diseases and Dangerous Occurrences Regulations 1995 (RIDDOR) require the 'responsible person' to notify any death, reportable injury, disease or dangerous occurrence to the relevant enforcing authority. The responsible person is the employer or, for the self-employed, the contractor or principal contractor.

Additional duties for notifiable projects

187 In the case of notifiable projects, contractors must also:

(a)   check that a CDM co-ordinator has been appointed and HSE notified before they start work (having a copy of the notification of the project to HSE (form 10, see paragraph 18), is normally sufficient);

(b)   co-operate with the principal contractor, CDM co-ordinator and others working on the project or adjacent sites;

(c)   tell the principal contractor about risks to others created by their work;

Regulation 19(2)(d)

(d)   provide details to the principal contractor of any contractor whom he engages in connection with carrying out the work;

(e)   comply with any reasonable directions from the principal contractor, and with any relevant rules in the construction phase plan;

(f)   inform the principal contractor of any problems with the plan or risks identified during their work that have significant implications for the management of the project;

(g)   tell the principal contractor about accidents and dangerous occurrences;

(h)   provide information for the health and safety file (see paragraphs 256-268).

188   Contractors must co-operate with the principal contractor, and assist them in the development of the construction phase plan and its implementation. Where contractors identify shortcomings in the plan, the contractor should inform the principal contractor.

189   On notifiable sites, contractors must promptly inform the principal contractor about risks to other site workers or members of the public resulting from their work. This includes anything, for example from risk assessments and written systems of work, which might justify a review or update of the construction phase plan. Contractors must also provide details to the principal contractor of any other contractors who they engage to assist in the carrying out of the work. Principal contractors must be in a position to know who is working on the site. Principal contractors also have duties relating to the provision of information to contractors, and they will not be in a position to discharge these duties if they are not told that such contractors have been engaged.

190   Contractors must also provide information about RIDDOR incidents to principal contractors so that they can monitor compliance with health and safety law and, if necessary, review the arrangements for the management of health and safety.

191   On notifiable projects, site induction should be provided by the principal contractor, but the contractor must co-operate with the principal contractor to ensure that an adequate site induction is provided.

192   Where contractors are involved in design work, including for temporary works, they also have duties as designers (see paragraphs 109-145.)

Regulation 19(2)(d)

ACOP

Regulation 19(2)(d)

Competence and training

193 This section gives advice about assessing the competence of organisations and individuals engaged or appointed under CDM2007 – CDM co-ordinators; designers; principal contractors and contractors.

194 **Assessments should focus on the needs of the particular project and be proportionate to the risks, size and complexity of the work.**

195 To be competent, an organisation or individual must have:

(a) sufficient knowledge of the specific tasks to be undertaken and the risks which the work will entail;

(b) sufficient experience and ability to carry out their duties in relation to the project; to recognise their limitations and take appropriate action in order to prevent harm to those carrying out construction work, or those affected by the work.

196 Organisations and individuals will need specific knowledge about the tasks they will be expected to perform, and the risks associated with these tasks. This will usually come from formal or 'on the job' training.

197 Appropriate experience is also a vital ingredient of competence. People are more likely to adopt safe working practices if they understand the reasons why they are necessary, and past experience should be a good indicator of the person's/company's track record.

198 The development of competence is an ongoing process. Individuals will develop their competence through experience in the job and through training which is part of 'life-long learning'. Professionals such as designers, CDM co-ordinators and advisors should be signed up to a 'Continuing Professional Development' programme either through their company or professional institution. This will allow them to remain 'up to date' with changes in legislation and professional practice. Construction trades workers and labourers should also receive refresher training or regular training updates either through an in-house planned programme of learning and development, or a more formal skills-based training programme such as those offered by the CITB Construction Skills.

ACOP

What you must do

199 All those with duties under CDM2007 must satisfy themselves that businesses that they engage or appoint are competent. This means making reasonable enquiries to check that the organisation or individual is competent to do the relevant work and can allocate adequate resources to it. Those taken on to do the work must also be sure that they are competent to carry out the required tasks before agreeing to take on the work.

200 For notifiable projects, a key duty of the CDM co-ordinator is to advise clients about competence of designers and contractors, including the principal contractor that they engage.

Regulation 4

201 **Doing an assessment requires you to make a judgement as to whether the organisation or individual has the competence to carry out the work safely. If your judgement is reasonable, taking into account the evidence that has been asked for and provided, you will not be criticised if the organisation you appoint subsequently proves not to have been competent to carry out the work.**

How to assess the competence of organisations

202 Competency assessments of organisations (including principal contractors, contractors, designers and CDM co-ordinators) should be carried out as a two-stage process:

203 **Stage 1**: An assessment of the company's organisation and arrangements for health and safety to determine whether these are sufficient to enable them to carry out the work safely and without risk to health.

204 **Stage 2**: An assessment of the company's experience and track record to establish that it is capable of doing the work; it recognises its limitations and how these should be overcome and it appreciates the risks from doing the work and how these should be tackled.

205 In order to provide more consistency in the way in which competency assessments of companies are carried out, a set of 'core criteria' have been agreed by industry and HSE. These are set out in Appendix 4. **Stage 1 and Stage 2 assessments should be made against these core criteria.**

206 Organisations who are bidding for work should put together a package of information that shows how their own policy, organisation and arrangements meet these standards. If regularly updated, this information should then be used each time they are asked to demonstrate competence as part of a tender process.

Example 20

A principal contractor engaged a roofing company, with whom they had worked before, to carry out refurbishment work on the roof of an existing warehouse. Competence checks were made, and these were cross-referenced with the performance of the roofing firm on the previous contracts. The contract was awarded, but the roofing firm sub-let the work to another company at a considerably reduced price. The company, which carried out the work, had never done such a large job before and was not competent to do the job.

A worker from this company fell to his death from the roof. The principal contractor and the roofing firm were each prosecuted for failing to adequately check the competence of the company which actually carried out the work.

207 Alternatively, organisations may use an independent accreditation organisation to assess their competence against the elements of the core criteria. Where this route is adopted, both clients (with the help of the CDM co-ordinator for notifiable projects) and organisations putting themselves forward for assessment should satisfy themselves that the accreditation body is using the criteria in Appendix 4 as a basis for the assessment, and that the assessment process is robust enough to give the assurance necessary to ensure compliance. Relevant trade associations should be able to advise you on which schemes are suitable.

208 Companies employing less than five people may not have a written health and safety policy, organisation and arrangements, but they do need to demonstrate that their policy, organisation and arrangements are adequate in relation to the type of work they do. This could be done through an oral briefing, but assessments of competence will be made easier if procedures are clear and accessible. **For small companies the assessment should be simple and straightforward, and they should be able to show that they meet the criteria without the need for extensive paperwork.**

209 Similarly, for smaller projects such as those falling below the notification threshold, companies should only be asked to provide the minimum paperwork necessary to show that they meet each element set out in the core criteria. For larger projects, or those where the risks are greater, a more in-depth assessment will be needed, but the assessment should not stray beyond the elements set out in the core criteria.

210 Where the project is much larger than any that the organisation being assessed has worked on before, or where the work will involve them managing new risks, this should not automatically rule them out for consideration for the work. The assessor should look for an appreciation of these risks; an understanding of how they will be managed, and some indication of how any shortcomings in their current arrangements for managing such risks will be addressed.

211 It may be that an organisation is weak in certain areas. This can be addressed by putting arrangements in place to cover these weaknesses, or by employing people with particular expertise for relevant parts of the contract. What really matters is that the organisation has access to the expertise which it needs, and the ability to control the risks which arise from the work.

212 Remember that assessments should focus on the needs of the particular project and be proportionate to the risks, size and complexity of the work. Unnecessary bureaucracy associated with competency assessment can obscure the real issues and divert effort away from them.

How to assess the competence of individuals

213 The information in this section will help clients, CDM co-ordinators or others who control the way in which construction work is carried out to assess the competence of key individuals. When assessing the competence of an organisation or company using the core criteria in Appendix 4, element 5 requires an assessment of individuals' qualifications and experience. The advice given in this section should be used to carry out such assessments.

214 Remember that assessments should focus on the needs of the particular job and should be proportionate to the risks arising from the work.

215 As with organisations, assessing the competence of an individual should be a two-stage process:

(a) **Stage 1**: An assessment of the person's task knowledge to determine whether this is sufficient to enable them to carry out the work safely and without risk to health;

(b) **Stage 2**: An assessment of the individual's experience and track record to establish that they are capable of doing the work; they recognise their limitations and how these should be overcome and they appreciate the risks from doing the work and how these should be controlled.

216 Stage 1 assessments will look at an individual's qualifications and training records, and arrangements which have been made for their Continuing Professional Development or lifelong learning. **This will include an assessment as to whether the individual has a basic understanding of the risks arising from construction work which is essential for all people who work on or regularly visit sites.**

217 Stage 2 assessments should concentrate on the person's past experience in the type of work which you are asking them to do. Where the work is more complex than any that the person has done before, or where the work will expose them to new risks, this should not automatically rule them out for consideration for the work. In these circumstances, the assessor should look for an appreciation of these risks; an understanding of how they will be managed, and some indication of how any shortcomings in their current knowledge will be addressed. Working under the supervision of someone who is competent and familiar with the work is one way in which people can learn how to do work safely.

Assessing an individual's basic understanding of site risks

218 A basic understanding of the general risks arising from construction work is essential underpinning knowledge for everyone who works in the industry in order that they can protect their own health and safety and understand the effect that their own actions could have on others. This is particularly important for those who will regularly visit or work on construction sites. This basic understanding should be the foundation for health and safety knowledge and understanding on which more detailed competencies are developed.

219 The CITB Construction Skills touch screen test and equivalent schemes such as that offered by the Construction Clients National Certification Scheme are designed specifically to test this basic knowledge and understanding. Passing the touch screen test or equivalent schemes is one way of demonstrating this basic knowledge and understanding. All those who work on or regularly visit sites (including individuals from client, designer or CDM co-ordinator organisations) should be able to demonstrate that they have achieved at least this level of understanding before starting work on site.

220 Those who are new to construction work will need close supervision by an experienced person until they can demonstrate that they are aware of these risks and know how to avoid harm.

Assessing the competence of individual designers and CDM co-ordinators

221 When carrying out an assessment for designers or CDM co-ordinators, membership of a relevant construction-related professional institution gives a strong indication that the person has the necessary task knowledge and experience needed to fulfil the role. Some institutions have different levels of membership which may give a clearer indication of the knowledge which they possess. Fellowship of an institution generally indicates that a member has more in-depth knowledge and experience of a subject than that held by an ordinary member. Membership of a particular register operated by an institution also helps to indicate areas in which a person has particular expertise, for example membership of the Health and Safety Register operated by the Institution of Civil Engineers (ICE), membership of the design register or CDM co-ordinators' register operated by the Association for Project Safety (APS), or membership of the CDM co-ordinators' register administered by the Institution of Construction Safety (ICS) (formerly the Institution of Planning Supervisors (IPS)).

Competence of individual designers

222 Membership of a relevant professional institution for example CIBSE; ICE; IMechE; IStructE; RIBA; RICS; CIAT; CIOB is a strong indicator that a designer has the necessary task knowledge and an ability to recognise the health and safety implications of their design work. Membership of a relevant register administered

ACOP

by such an institution gives a more detailed indication that the designer has the necessary knowledge and experience, for example the Construction Health and Safety Register of the ICE, or the design register operated by the APS.

223 Those who specify materials, equipment and standards of finish (for example interior designers) are also considered designers under the Regulations, but they tend not to be members of specific professional institutions. Relevant academic qualifications or evidence of their past experience in this type of work will give a strong indicator as to their competence.

224 Those who only occasionally become involved with design work and who do not meet the qualifying criteria (for example trainees) should work under the supervision of a competent designer.

225 When carrying out **Stage 2** of the assessment you should consider the designer's past experience in the type of work which you are asking them to do. Those without relevant experience should be allowed to work under the supervision of someone who has it. If designers work as part of a team, different individuals may bring different skills and knowledge to the work, and this should be taken into account when making the assessment.

Assessing the competence of individual CDM co-ordinators

226 CDM co-ordinators need good interpersonal skills in order to encourage co-operation between designers and others. Although there is a legal duty to co-operate on everyone involved with the project, the CDM co-ordinator has a specific duty to ensure that co-operation happens. Without it, good working relationships, clear communication and sharing of relevant information will not happen. An over-bureaucratic approach should be avoided, not least because it makes it harder to secure the co-operation which is needed.

227 CDM co-ordinators also need a sound understanding of:

(a) health and safety in construction work;

(b) the design process;

(c) the importance of co-ordination of the design process, and an ability to identify information which others will need to know about the design in order to carry out their work safely.

228 This knowledge needs to be relevant to the project and future maintenance, use, refurbishment or demolition of the structure. The size and complexity of the project will determine whether an individual is capable, and has the resources to carry out all of the work required.

229 CDM co-ordinators are not necessarily designers, and do not have to undertake any design work themselves. But in order to assess the health and safety implications of the design, they must have sufficient knowledge of the design process to enable them to hold meaningful discussions with designers, recognise when information about risks arising from the design will need to be passed to others and participate fully in relevant design team meetings. They will also need to be in a position to advise clients about the competence of others who are appointed by the client, and be able to assess whether the construction phase plan prepared by the principal contractor is adequate for controlling the risks associated with the project.

Regulation 4

ACOP

230 When carrying out the assessment, clients will need to take into account the size and complexity of the project, and the nature of the risks which will be associated with it. Where one individual does not possess all of the skills and experience necessary, the work can be shared with others, but it must be clear who is responsible for each part of the work, and who is in overall control.

231 For small projects where there are no special risks, **Stage 1** of the assessment should concentrate on the person's knowledge of the construction processes and the health and safety risks associated with the work. An appropriate health and safety qualification such as a NEBOSH construction certificate will demonstrate that the person has adequate knowledge of health and safety, but this will need to be coupled with a **Stage 2** assessment to demonstrate that they have experience in applying this knowledge in the construction environment. Registration on the CDM co-ordinators' register administered by the ICS (formerly the IPS) or the APS or membership of the Health and Safety Register administered by the ICE can be taken as confirmation that the person has the necessary task knowledge and experience to carry out the CDM co-ordinator's duties on this type of project.

232 For larger or more complex projects, or for those with unusual or higher risks, the skills and knowledge of the CDM co-ordinator will need to reflect the complexity of the project and the specialist knowledge necessary to ensure that risks are properly controlled. It is more likely in these circumstances that a corporate appointment will be made and the competence assessment will be made against the core criteria mentioned in paragraph 205. The table in Appendix 5 gives further guidance on the standards to be achieved for CDM co-ordinators appointed to this type of project.

233 CDM co-ordinators cannot carry out their duties effectively without the client's support. For that reason they will often need an understanding of relevant aspects of the client's business and the implications of the proposed work for it. CDM co-ordinators will need to make sure that clients understand their own role and duties as well as the benefits of good management of the project and early appointment of dutyholders.

Regulation 4

ACOP

Assessing the competence of an individual site worker

234 Employers are required by law to ensure the competence of their employees and to provide training and instruction as necessary. CDM2007 places duties on contractors and principal contractors to ensure that workers are competent and to provide training where necessary.

235 As explained in paragraph 219, an appropriate Skills for Business Organisation, or similar programme give a good indication of this basic knowledge and understanding. This should be the foundation for health and safety knowledge and understanding on which more detailed competencies are developed.

236 Having gained this basic knowledge and understanding, workers should then receive regular updates and more specialised training as part of a life-long learning process. This should either be delivered through a planned programme of 'on-the-job' training, for example through regular on-site 'toolbox' talks coupled with 'off-the-job' training days, or through a more formal, assessed training package, for example an S/NVQ programme administered by an appropriate Skills for Business organisation, or similar programme.

Regulations 4, 13(4) and (5) and 22(2)

237 The chart at Appendix 6 shows a typical timeline for an unskilled construction worker from their first job in construction to a point where they can

ACOP

be considered competent. Workers who follow the 'in-house training' route to competence will need to ensure that the training they receive covers the health and safety aspects of the job as well as the necessary skills elements. Those who enrol on an accredited S/NVQ course will receive both elements of the training as part of the assessed course.

238 Unskilled workers who are following a programme of training will, over time, gather the necessary competence to become a skilled worker. With further experience and training, they should gain the competence necessary to become a supervisor. The table below summarises the knowledge, skills and likely capabilities of a typical trainee, a skilled worker and a supervisor.

239 When developing training schemes, it is important to ensure that the content and style are appropriate. This includes providing training in a form that trainees can understand. Workforce or trade union appointed safety representatives can make a significant contribution to developing such training, and a joint approach can help ensure people adopt good practices. Information and training should be provided in a way that takes account of any language difficulties or disabilities further advice is provided by CILT, the National Centre for Languages (www.cilt.org.uk) and the Construction Confederation (www.thecc.org.uk). It can be provided in whatever form is most suitable in the circumstances, as long as it can be understood by everyone. For employees with little or no understanding of spoken or written English, employers need to make special arrangements. These include providing translation, using interpreters, and replacing written notices with clear symbols or diagrams.

Regulations 4, 13(4) and (5) and 22(2)

240 Further information about training opportunities available to construction workers can be found from www.constructionskills.net or www.summitskills.org.uk.

Management responsibility

The right person for the right job			
Level	The job	Training and supervision	Measuring performance
Trainee	Carry out a risk assessment and as a result: Specify the tasks for the trainee; the tools, PPE and equipment; the limits of activity; the procedures to learn; assign to a supervisor; spell out the behaviour expected.	Provide supervision according to the risk assessment; provide induction training; train to pass the CITB-CS health and safety test; provide support to learn procedures and behaviours.	Set training targets and check regularly to see if these are achieved; monitor the performance and behaviours of both supervisor and trainee.
Site worker	Specify tasks; authorise use of plant, equipment etc according to qualifications and experience; communicate site rules for consultation co-operation.	Check qualifications, provide induction training, ongoing development and support to learn site-wide procedures and play a full part in consultation.	Carry out regular observations of performance against standards and site rules; encourage best practice, use management procedures which correctly reward good practice and deter bad practice.
Supervisor	Specify the standards that supervisors should be achieving, particularly on consultation and behaviour expectations.	Check qualifications; set up a reporting chain; provide management and technical support; provide training and development on management issues as required.	Performance agreement with supervisor correctly identifies and rewards health and safety elements; monitor implementation of management procedures by supervisors.

Individual competence

Trainee		
	Description	Example of attainment
Risk control knowledge	Adequate knowledge of tasks to be undertaken; understands what is expected and when to ask for help; understands role and importance of supervisor; can identify key risks of activities; knows how to react to basic risks; knows main health hazards and why PPE is important.	CITB-CS Health and Safety Test or CCNSG Certificate or equivalent recognised passport training S/NVQ Level 1.
Experience and ability	From no experience; has physical capability to carry out duties; minimum standard of language skills; can identify deteriorating conditions which may lead to increased risk; is aware of personal responsibility for him or herself and others, is aware of what constitutes a good attitude.	Attends site induction; attends mandatory in-house training; works safely to agreed standard under supervision; demonstrates safe behaviour and wears appropriate PPE at all times.

Site worker		
	Description	Example of attainment
Risk control knowledge	As for trainee, plus: knows standards of health and safety required for site operations; can identify all foreseeable risks arising from their work activity and know what actions to take to control these risks; can apply existing knowledge to new circumstances.	As for trainee, plus: S/NVQ Level 2 or 3.
Experience and ability	As for trainee, plus: consistently works to agreed standards of health and safety; quickly identifies defects and unacceptable risks; demonstrates good attitude and example at work; capable of working safely with minimal supervision.	As for trainee, plus: commensurate with Level 2 achievement; plays full role in site consultation; demonstrates ability to report unsafe conditions to supervisor; demonstrates motivation to learn.

Supervisor		
	Description	Example of attainment
Risk control knowledge	As for site worker plus: knows how to lead in identifying remedial actions to mitigate risk in all foreseeable circumstances; understands implications of his or her own decisions on others; knows when to ask for specialist help.	As for site worker plus: S/NVQ Level 3. Knowledge of supervision equivalent to CITB-CS 2-day supervisors' course, NEBOSH certificate etc.
Experience and ability	Able to identify causes of problems and to deploy resources to solve problems on own initiative; demonstrates leadership skills, appropriate communication strategies; can read plans, think through problems and is flexible to adapt to changing circumstances.	3-5 years' experience of this operation; trained and qualified to a level where he can describe risks of the range of work activities he is responsible for, is capable of identifying remote risks, and anticipating problems of change.

Worker engagement and communication

ACOP

241 Involving the workforce in identifying and controlling risks is crucial to reducing the high accident rate associated with construction work. The workforce has first-hand experience of site conditions and is often the first to identify potential problems. Worker engagement is the participation by workers in decisions made by those in control of construction activities, in order that risks on site can be managed in the most effective way.

242 Participation will be most effective when the workforce has sufficient knowledge and confidence to provide feedback, and can identify risks and explain their importance. People have the confidence to do this when they are properly trained, know how to report their concerns, and see prompt action being taken as a result. Training should include, where necessary, the skills required to participate in decision-making processes, and consultation with managers.

Regulations 4, 13(4) and (5) and 22(2)

ACOP

What you are required to do for all projects

Providing information

243 All those in control of construction work are required to provide workers (including the self-employed) under their control with any information that worker needs to carry out the construction work safely and without risk to health.

> **Example 21**
>
> A major contractor recognised that for a site operative to fully participate in management meetings on health and safety, certain skills were needed. For example to know how to prioritise issues, how to present an evidence-based argument for change and how to judge what is a reasonable and constructive response from a manager. Training on this site was provided to safety representatives, both trade union recognised and non-trade union, through a site-based TUC-recognised training course for safety representatives.

244 All workers should be provided with a suitable site-specific induction to inform them of the arrangements for health, safety and welfare at their work site. This should include any relevant findings resulting from a risk assessment, including risks arising from the activities of other workers working nearby. If contractors have site rules these should be explained, along with the procedures to be followed in the event of any worker finding themselves in a position of serious and imminent danger. Contractors must communicate to their workers the identity of the person who is responsible for implementing health and safety procedures on site. Every worker has a duty under CDM to report anything, which is likely to endanger the health and safety of himself or others.

245 To ensure involvement of the entire workforce, contractors may need to make special arrangements for workers who have little or no understanding of English, or who cannot read English. These could include providing translation, using interpreters or replacing written notices with clearly understood symbols or diagrams.

246 Arrangements for worker engagement on smaller sites should always be tailored to the size and nature of the project and risks involved. On smaller sites informal arrangements for collecting workers' views can be effective. An effective way of achieving this is to arrange reviews of method statements immediately before the work itself is being carried out. Those workers who will be involved in the work can then comment directly on the risks and the ways in which these are being controlled.

Regulations 5(2) and 13(4)

ACOP

Example 22

A medium-sized contractor uses the site induction as an opportunity, not only to communicate messages to the workers attending, but also to involve those workers in initial discussion on health and safety matters. The contractor recognises induction as a first opportunity to make a strong impression on workers, but also to assess individual attitudes and competence.

Worker representatives

247 Employers must consult their workers on matters relating to their health and safety. This can often be done most effectively through worker representatives. Health and safety law recognises two types of worker representative:

(a) those appointed by recognised trade unions under the Safety Representatives and Safety Committees Regulations 1977[5] (SRSCR); and,

(b) representatives of employee safety elected by the workforce under the Health and Safety (Consultation with Employees) Regulations 1996[6] (HSCER).

Both types of representative are entitled to paid time off to discharge their functions and for training to enable them to play a full and active part in securing health and safety. In the case of representatives under the 1996 Regulations, this training must be paid for by their employer. Suitable training is available through a number of organisations, including trade unions.

Regulations 5(2) and 13(4)

ACOP

Arrangements for serious and imminent danger

248 Regulation 8 of the Management of Health and Safety at Work Regulations 1999 requires employers to establish and give effect, where necessary, to appropriate procedures to be followed in the event of serious and imminent danger to persons at work. It also enables any worker exposed to serious and imminent danger to stop work and immediately proceed to a place of safety. Contractors should consult with the workforce to ensure that all workers are aware of this right, and that they have procedures in place to effectively deal with these situations when they arise. Serious and imminent danger means that the risk of injury or ill health is serious, and that the danger will arise as soon as the work would begin.

Example 23

On a major new build project, managers were won over and reassured by the style and no-nonsense approach adopted by the trade union appointed safety representative, who demonstrated a real commitment to safety, and a refusal to get sidetracked by issues with no relevance to health and safety.

In an alternative approach a principal contractor appointed and trained a senior employee in his late fifties to act as a safety coach, operating outside the normal line management chain, to walk the sites, supporting and encouraging the workers to adopt and maintain high standards of health and safety. The client was supportive of this role, which has now expanded in this company.

Regulation 13(4)(e)

052428

ACOP

Additional arrangements for notifiable projects

Co-operation and consultation

249 In addition to the duties outlined above, principal contractors have the specific duties to make and maintain arrangements to enable effective co-operation and consultation between themselves, contractors and workers.

> **Example 24**
>
> Directors of a specialist sub-contractor committed themselves to visiting all their company's ten sites in a three-month period and speaking to every operative. Their simple message was 'Look after yourself, do not take shortcuts'.
>
> Alongside this, four hot topics were identified, including respect for people, housekeeping, pedestrian walkways and site planning. Toolbox talks were given setting out the company's standards on these topics and engaging individual workers in discussion. Managers demonstrated commitment by allocating resources to these topics, and encouraging zero tolerance to lower standards.

250 Worker engagement requires principal contractors to encourage collaboration and trust between contractors on their sites. This goes much further than simply consulting workers on issues such as what kind of wet weather clothing they would find most useful. It involves a joint commitment to solving problems together. Effective worker engagement will develop from effective consultation and co-operation between the principal contractor and other contractors on site. Effective worker engagement by a principal contractor will include the following three elements:

(a) a commitment by managers to lead by example, to provide the resources, targets and expectations to make the process work;

(b) implementation of a range of mechanisms to communicate, ensure co-operation with and consult the workforce in managing health and safety on site;

(c) collecting the evidence that the mechanisms are effective, that the workforce is involved, and that co-operation between contractors is successful.

Co-operation

251 Principal contractors should record the arrangements they make for co-operation and consultation with workers on their site in the construction phase plan. These arrangements will require regular review and updating, as the circumstances on site change. The arrangements need to cover all workers effectively, including those who may only be on site for brief periods. The arrangements should be proportionate to the size and complexity of the construction work, the scale of the hazards and the size of the workforce. The workforce and their representatives should contribute to the development of this plan; and, in particular, to provide insights into specialised areas of activity.

Regulation 24

ACOP

Regulation 24

Example 25

A principal contractor established daily briefings from supervisors to the gang under their control. These supervisors covered a range of trades and employers. Managers cascaded the information supervisors needed to ensure risks in their part of the worksite are identified and controlled, including those risks created where different activities took place in close proximity. Supervisors completed a card indicating who had received the briefing, with space for feedback to the principal contractor on any matters arising.

The principal contractor showed commitment to the system by monitoring every card completed, taking remedial action, and by following up when cards were not completed.

252 All the dutyholders on site should respond positively and constructively to initiatives proposed and implemented by the principal contractor. The principal contractor has a duty to plan ahead, to foresee particular periods in the construction schedule where the workforce may be particularly busy, and to take these into account. Principal contractors may develop a range of solutions to improve co-operation on site. For example:

(a)   involving workers in carrying out site-specific risk assessments;

(b)   setting up clearly defined communication channels, to alert the workforce to developments on site;

(c)   briefing sub-contractors regularly on the work programme;

(d)   requiring regular, or daily briefings where front line supervisors brief workers on the work programme and day-to-day risks on site;

(e)   setting up formal committees or operatives forums;

(f)   ensuring that issues raised are dealt with and feedback is provided to the workforce.

253 Principal contractors have a duty to monitor the effectiveness of the measures they take to ensure the health and safety of workers on their sites. The emphasis should be on obtaining simple feedback, avoiding the need for workers themselves to fill in forms.

Example 26

On a major new hospital site, the principal contractor established a mixed safety committee where TU-appointed safety representatives sat alongside non-union representatives from smaller sub-contractors. Training was provided for these representatives on site, and once established, the committee increasingly addressed significant health and safety issues, moving away from complaints about welfare to discussions about improving logistics and planning through better communication and co-operation. The committee recognised that meaningful consultation requires training, planning and thoughtful contributions from workers and managers, with a real commitment to improving standards through joint problem-solving.

ACOP

Consultation

254 Individual employers have a duty to consult with their own employees on matters that affect their health and safety. CDM2007 places additional duties on the principal contractor to consult with all workers involved in a project, to ensure that the measures taken to protect workers' health and safety are effective.

255 Consultation means not only giving information to workers, but also listening and taking account of what workers say, before making health and safety decisions. Principal contractors do not have to duplicate consultation, which an employer has already carried out, for example on the detail of a contractor's method statement. Principal contractors should implement a range of mechanisms to ensure that consultation is effective. Possible ways of doing this include:

(a) engaging with representatives of the workforce (whether appointed by a recognised trade union or elected by the workforce);

(b) establishing health and safety committees or forums;

(c) regular consultation meetings;

(d) consultation during inductions, daily briefings, toolbox talks, site-wide meetings;

(e) informal methods, for example during site managers' walkabouts, or during senior managers' visits;

Regulation 24

(f) procedures to encourage workers to report defects, deterioration in conditions or innovations to raise standards.

ACOP

The health and safety file (notifiable projects only)

256 The health and safety file should contain the information needed to allow future construction work, including cleaning, maintenance, alterations, refurbishment and demolition to be carried out safely. Information in the file should alert those carrying out such work to risks, and should help them to decide how to work safely. The file should be useful to:

(a) clients, who have a duty to provide information about their premises to those who carry out work there;

(b) designers during the development of further designs or alterations;

(c) CDM co-ordinators preparing for construction work;

(d) principal contractors and contractors preparing to carry out or manage such work.

257 The file should form a key part of the information that the client, or the client's successor, is required to provide for future construction projects under regulation 10. The file should therefore be kept up to date after any relevant work or surveys.

258 **The scope, structure and format for the file should be agreed between the client and CDM co-ordinator at the start of a project.** There can be a separate file for each structure, one for an entire project or site, or one for a group of related structures. The file may be combined with the Building Regulations Log Book, or a maintenance manual providing that this does not result in the health and safety information being lost or buried. What matters is that people can find the information they need easily and that any differences between similar structures are clearly shown.

Regulation 24

ACOP

What you must do

259 Clients, designers, principal contractors, other contractors and CDM co-ordinators all have legal duties in respect of the health and safety file:

(a) CDM co-ordinators must prepare, review, amend or add to the file as the project progresses, and give it to the client at the end of project;

(b) clients, designers, principal contractors and other contractors must supply the information necessary for compiling or updating the file;

(c) clients must keep the file to assist with future construction work; and

(d) everyone providing information should make sure that it is accurate, and provided promptly.

260 A file must be produced or updated (if one already exists) as part of all notifiable projects. For some projects, for example redecoration using non-toxic materials, there may be nothing of substance to record. Only information likely to be significant for health and safety in future work need be included. The NHBC Purchaser Manual provides suitable information for developers to give to householders. You do not have to produce a file on the whole structure if a project only involves a small amount of construction work on part of the structure.

Regulations 17, 20(1)(c) and (2)(e)

ACOP

Regulation 17(3)
and (4)

267 In multi-occupancy situations, for example where a housing association owns a block of flats, the owner should keep and maintain the file, but ensure that individual flat occupiers are supplied with health and safety information concerning their home.

268 A development may include roads and sewers that will be adopted by the local authority or water company. It is generally best to prepare separate files covering each client's interests.

Appendix 1

The Construction (Design and Management) Regulations 2007

PART 1 INTRODUCTION

Regulation 1

Citation and commencement

These Regulations may be cited as the Construction (Design and Management) Regulations 2007 and shall come into force on 6th April 2007.

Regulation 2

Interpretation

(1) In these Regulations, unless the context otherwise requires—
"business" means a trade, business or other undertaking (whether for profit or not);

"client" means a person who in the course or furtherance of a business—

(a) seeks or accepts the services of another which may be used in the carrying out of a project for him; or

(b) carries out a project himself;

"CDM co-ordinator" means the person appointed as the CDM co-ordinator under regulation 14(1);

"construction site" includes any place where construction work is being carried out or to which the workers have access, but does not include a workplace within it which is set aside for purposes other than construction work;

"construction phase" means the period of time starting when construction work in any project starts and ending when construction work in that project is completed;

"construction phase plan" means a document recording the health and safety arrangements, site rules and any special measures for construction work;

"construction work" means the carrying out of any building, civil engineering or engineering construction work and includes—

(a) the construction, alteration, conversion, fitting out, commissioning, renovation, repair, upkeep, redecoration or other maintenance (including cleaning which involves the use of water or an abrasive at high pressure or the use of corrosive or toxic substances), de-commissioning, demolition or dismantling of a structure;

(b) the preparation for an intended structure, including site clearance, exploration, investigation (but not site survey) and excavation, and the clearance or preparation of the site or structure for use or occupation at its conclusion;

(c) the assembly on site of prefabricated elements to form a structure or the disassembly on site of prefabricated elements which, immediately before such disassembly, formed a structure;

(d)   the removal of a structure or of any product or waste resulting from demolition or dismantling of a structure or from disassembly of prefabricated elements which immediately before such disassembly formed such a structure; and

(e)   the installation, commissioning, maintenance, repair or removal of mechanical, electrical, gas, compressed air, hydraulic, telecommunications, computer or similar services which are normally fixed within or to a structure,

but does not include the exploration for or extraction of mineral resources or activities preparatory thereto carried out at a place where such exploration or extraction is carried out;

"contractor" means any person (including a client, principal contractor or other person referred to in these Regulations) who, in the course or furtherance of a business, carries out or manages construction work;

"design" includes drawings, design details, specification and bill of quantities (including specification of articles or substances) relating to a structure, and calculations prepared for the purpose of a design;

"designer" means any person (including a client, contractor or other person referred to in these Regulations) who in the course or furtherance of a business—

(a)   prepares or modifies a design; or

(b)   arranges for or instructs any person under his control to do so,

relating to a structure or to a product or mechanical or electrical system intended for a particular structure, and a person is deemed to prepare a design where a design is prepared by a person under his control;

"excavation" includes any earthwork, trench, well, shaft, tunnel or underground working;

"the Executive" means the Health and Safety Executive;

"the general principles of prevention" means the general principles of prevention specified in Schedule 1 to the Management of Health and Safety at Work Regulations 1999[a]

"health and safety file"—

(a)   means the record referred to in regulation 20(2)(e); and

(b)   includes a health and safety file prepared under regulation 14(d) of the Construction (Design and Management) Regulations 1994[b];

"loading bay" means any facility for loading or unloading;

(a) S.I. 1999/3242, to which there are amendments not relevant to these Regulations.
(b) S.I. 1994/3140, amended by S.I. 2006/557; there are other amending instruments but none is relevant.

"place of work" means any place which is used by any person at work for the purposes of construction work or for the purposes of any activity arising out of or in connection with construction work;

"pre-construction information" means the information described in regulation 10 and, where the project is notifiable, regulation 15.

"principal contractor" means the person appointed as the principal contractor under regulation 14(2);

"project" means a project which includes or is intended to include construction work and includes all planning, design, management or other work involved in a project until the end of the construction phase;

"site rules" means the rules described in regulation 22(1)(d);

"structure" means—

    (a)   any building, timber, masonry, metal or reinforced concrete structure, railway line or siding, tramway line, dock, harbour, inland navigation, tunnel, shaft, bridge, viaduct, waterworks, reservoir, pipe or pipe-line, cable, aqueduct, sewer, sewage works, gasholder, road, airfield, sea defence works, river works, drainage works, earthworks, lagoon, dam, wall, caisson, mast, tower, pylon, underground tank, earth retaining structure or structure designed to preserve or alter any natural feature, fixed plant and any structure similar to the foregoing; or

    (b)   any formwork, falsework, scaffold or other structure designed or used to provide support or means of access during construction work,

and any reference to a structure includes a part of a structure.

"traffic route" means a route for pedestrian traffic or for vehicles and includes any doorway, gateway, loading bay or ramp;

"vehicle" includes any mobile work equipment;

"work equipment" means any machinery, appliance, apparatus, tool or installation for use at work (whether exclusively or not);

"workplace" means a workplace within the meaning of regulation 2(1) of the Workplace (Health, Safety and Welfare) Regulations 1992[(a)] other than a construction site; and

"writing" includes writing which is kept in electronic form and which can be printed.

    (2)   Any reference in these Regulations to a plan, rules, document, report or copy includes a plan, rules, document, report or copy which is kept in a form—

    (a)   in which it is capable of being reproduced as a printed copy when required; and

    (b)   which is secure from loss or unauthorised interference.

(a) S.I. 1992/3004, amended by S.I. 2002/2174 and S.I. 2005/735; there are other amending instruments but none is relevant.

<table>
<tr><td>

Regulation

2
</td><td>

(3)   For the purposes of these Regulations, a project is notifiable if the construction phase is likely to involve more than—

(a)   30 days; or

(b)   500 person days,

of construction work.
</td></tr>
</table>

Regulation 3

<table>
<tr><td>

Regulation

3
</td><td>

Application

(1)   These Regulations shall apply—

(a)   in Great Britain; and

(b)   outside Great Britain as sections 1 to 59 and 80 to 82 of the 1974 Act apply by virtue of article 8(1)(a) of the Health and Safety at Work etc. Act 1974 (Application outside Great Britain) Order 2001[a].

(2)   Subject to the following paragraphs of this regulation, these Regulations shall apply to and in relation to construction work.

(3)   The duties under Part 3 shall apply only where a project—

(a)   is notifiable; and

(b)   is carried out for or on behalf of, or by, a client.

(4)   Part 4 shall apply only in relation to a construction site.

(5)   Regulations 9(1)(b), 13(7), 22(1)(c), and Schedule 2 shall apply only in relation to persons at work who are carrying out construction work.

(a) S.I. 2001/2127.
</td></tr>
</table>

PART 2 GENERAL MANAGEMENT DUTIES APPLYING TO CONSTRUCTION PROJECTS

Regulation 4

Regulation

4

Competence

(1)   *No person on whom these Regulations place a duty shall—*

(a)   *appoint or engage a CDM co-ordinator, designer, principal contractor or contractor unless he has taken reasonable steps to ensure that the person to be appointed or engaged is competent;*

(b)   *accept such an appointment or engagement unless he is competent;*

(c)   *arrange for or instruct a worker to carry out or manage design or construction work unless the worker is—*

(i)   *competent, or*

(ii)   *under the supervision of a competent person.*

(2)   *Any reference in this regulation to a person being competent shall extend only to his being competent to—*

(a)   *perform any requirement; and*

(b)   *avoid contravening any prohibition,*

imposed on him by or under any of the relevant statutory provisions.

Regulation 5

Regulation

5

Co-operation

(1)   *Every person concerned in a project on whom a duty is placed by these Regulations, including paragraph (2), shall—*

(a)   *seek the co-operation of any other person concerned in any project involving construction work at the same or an adjoining site so far as is necessary to enable himself to perform any duty or function under these Regulations; and*

(b)   *co-operate with any other person concerned in any project involving construction work at the same or an adjoining site so far as is necessary to enable that person to perform any duty or function under these Regulations.*

(2)   *Every person concerned in a project who is working under the control of another person shall report to that person anything which he is aware is likely to endanger the health or safety of himself or others.*

Regulation 6

Regulation

6

Co-ordination

All persons concerned in a project on whom a duty is placed by these Regulations shall co-ordinate their activities with one another in a manner which ensures, so far as is reasonably practicable, the health and safety of persons—

Regulation
6

(a)   carrying out the construction work; and

(b)   affected by the construction work.

Regulation 7

General principles of prevention

Regulation

7

(1)   Every person on whom a duty is placed by these Regulations in relation to the design, planning and preparation of a project shall take account of the general principles of prevention in the performance of those duties during all the stages of the project.

(2)   Every person on whom a duty is placed by these Regulations in relation to the construction phase of a project shall ensure so far as is reasonably practicable that the general principles of prevention are applied in the carrying out of the construction work.

Regulation 8

Election by clients

Regulation

8

Where there is more than one client in relation to a project, if one or more of such clients elect in writing to be treated for the purposes of these Regulations as the only client or clients, no other client who has agreed in writing to such election shall be subject after such election and consent to any duty owed by a client under these Regulations save the duties in regulations 5(1)(b), 10(1), 15 and 17(1) insofar as those duties relate to information in his possession.

Regulation 9

Client's duty in relation to arrangements for managing projects

Regulation

9

(1)   Every client shall take reasonable steps to ensure that the arrangements made for managing the project (including the allocation of sufficient time and other resources) by persons with a duty under these Regulations (including the client himself) are suitable to ensure that—

(a)   the construction work can be carried out so far as is reasonably practicable without risk to the health and safety of any person;

(b)   the requirements of Schedule 2 are complied with in respect of any person carrying out the construction work; and

(c)   any structure designed for use as a workplace has been designed taking account of the provisions of the Workplace (Health, Safety and Welfare) Regulations 1992 which relate to the design of, and materials used in, the structure.

(2)   The client shall take reasonable steps to ensure that the arrangements referred to in paragraph (1) are maintained and reviewed throughout the project.

Regulation 10

Client's duty in relation to information

Regulation

10

(1)   Every client shall ensure that

(a)   every person designing the structure; and

(b)   every contractor who has been or may be appointed by the client,

is promptly provided with pre-construction information in accordance with paragraph (2).

(2)   The pre-construction information shall consist of all the information in the client's possession (or which is reasonably obtainable), including—

(a)   any information about or affecting the site or the construction work;

(b)   any information concerning the proposed use of the structure as a workplace;

(c)   the minimum amount of time before the construction phase which will be allowed to the contractors appointed by the client for planning and preparation for construction work; and

(d)   any information in any existing health and safety file,

which is relevant to the person to whom the client provides it for the purposes specified in paragraph (3).

(3)   The purposes referred to in paragraph (2) are—

(a)   to ensure so far as is reasonably practicable the health and safety of persons—

(i)   engaged in the construction work,

(ii)   liable to be affected by the way in which it is carried out, and

(iii)   who will use the structure as a workplace; and

(b)   without prejudice to sub-paragraph (a), to assist the persons to whom information is provided under this regulation—

(i)   to perform their duties under these Regulations, and

(ii)   to determine the resources referred to in regulation 9(1) which they are to allocate for managing the project.

10

Regulation 11

Duties of designers

(1)   No designer shall commence work in relation to a project unless any client for the project is aware of his duties under these Regulations.

(2)   The duties in paragraphs (3) and (4) shall be performed so far as is reasonably practicable, taking due account of other relevant design considerations.

(3)   Every designer shall in preparing or modifying a design which may be used in construction work in Great Britain avoid foreseeable risks to the health and safety of any person—

(a)   carrying out construction work;

(b)   liable to be affected by such construction work;

11

Regulation

11

(c)   cleaning any window or any transparent or translucent wall, ceiling or roof in or on a structure;

(d)   maintaining the permanent fixtures and fittings of a structure; or

(e)   using a structure designed as a workplace.

(4)   In discharging the duty in paragraph (3), the designer shall—

(a)   eliminate hazards which may give rise to risks; and

(b)   reduce risks from any remaining hazards,

and in so doing shall give collective measures priority over individual measures.

(5)   In designing any structure for use as a workplace the designer shall take account of the provisions of the Workplace (Health, Safety and Welfare) Regulations 1992 which relate to the design of, and materials used in, the structure.

(6)   The designer shall take all reasonable steps to provide with his design sufficient information about aspects of the design of the structure or its construction or maintenance as will adequately assist—

(a)   clients;

(b)   other designers; and

(c)   contractors,

to comply with their duties under these Regulations.

Regulation 12

Designs prepared or modified outside Great Britain

Regulation

12

Where a design is prepared or modified outside Great Britain for use in construction work to which these Regulations apply—

(a)   the person who commissions it, if he is established within Great Britain; or

(b)   if that person is not so established, any client for the project,

shall ensure that regulation 11 is complied with.

Regulation 13

Duties of contractors

Regulation

13

(1)   No contractor shall carry out construction work in relation to a project unless any client for the project is aware of his duties under these Regulations.

(2)   Every contractor shall plan, manage and monitor construction work carried out by him or under his control in a way which ensures that, so far as is reasonably practicable, it is carried out without risks to health and safety.

(3)   Every contractor shall ensure that any contractor whom he appoints or engages in his turn in connection with a project is informed of the minimum

Regulation

amount of time which will be allowed to him for planning and preparation before he begins construction work.

(4)   Every contractor shall provide every worker carrying out the construction work under his control with any information and training which he needs for the particular work to be carried out safely and without risk to health, including—

(a)   suitable site induction, where not provided by any principal contractor;

(b)   information on the risks to their health and safety—

(i)   identified by his risk assessment under regulation 3 of the Management of Health and Safety at Work Regulations 1999, or

(ii)   arising out of the conduct by another contractor of his undertaking and of which he is or ought reasonably to be aware;

(c)   the measures which have been identified by the contractor in consequence of the risk assessment as the measures he needs to take to comply with the requirements and prohibitions imposed upon him by or under the relevant statutory provisions;

(d)   any site rules;

(e)   the procedures to be followed in the event of serious and imminent danger to such workers; and

(f)   the identity of the persons nominated to implement those procedures.

(5)   Without prejudice to paragraph (4), every contractor shall in the case of any of his employees provide those employees with any health and safety training which he is required to provide to them in respect of the construction work by virtue of regulation 13(2)(b) of the Management of Health and Safety at Work Regulations 1999.

(6)   No contractor shall begin work on a construction site unless reasonable steps have been taken to prevent access by unauthorised persons to that site.

(7)   Every contractor shall ensure, so far as is reasonably practicable, that the requirements of Schedule 2 are complied with throughout the construction phase in respect of any person at work who is under his control.

13

PART 3 ADDITIONAL DUTIES WHERE PROJECT IS NOTIFIABLE

Regulation 14

Appointments by the client where a project is notifiable

(1) Where a project is notifiable, the client shall appoint a person ("the CDM co-ordinator") to perform the duties specified in regulations 20 and 21 as soon as is practicable after initial design work or other preparation for construction work has begun.

(2) After appointing a CDM co-ordinator under paragraph (1), the client shall appoint a person ("the principal contractor") to perform the duties specified in regulations 22 to 24 as soon as is practicable after the client knows enough about the project to be able to select a suitable person for such appointment.

(3) The client shall ensure that appointments under paragraphs (1) and (2) are changed or renewed as necessary to ensure that there is at all times until the end of the construction phase a CDM co-ordinator and principal contractor.

(4) The client shall—

(a) be deemed for the purposes of these Regulations, save paragraphs (1) and (2) and regulations 18(1) and 19(1)(a) to have been appointed as the CDM co-ordinator or principal contractor, or both, for any period for which no person (including himself) has been so appointed; and

(b) accordingly be subject to the duties imposed by regulations 20 and 21 on a CDM co-ordinator or, as the case may be, the duties imposed by regulations 22 to 24 on a principal contractor, or both sets of duties.

(5) Any reference in this regulation to appointment is to appointment in writing.

14

Regulation 15

Client's duty in relation to information where a project is notifiable

Where the project is notifiable, the client shall promptly provide the CDM co-ordinator with pre-construction information consisting of—

(a) all the information described in regulation 10(2) to be provided to any person in pursuance of regulation 10(1);

(b) any further information as described in regulation 10(2) in the client's possession (or which is reasonably obtainable) which is relevant to the CDM co-ordinator for the purposes specified in regulation 10(3), including the minimum amount of time before the construction phase which will be allowed to the principal contractor for planning and preparation for construction work.

15

Regulation 16

Regulation

16

The client's duty in relation to the start of the construction phase where a project is notifiable

Where the project is notifiable, the client shall ensure that the construction phase does not start unless—

(a) *the principal contractor has prepared a construction phase plan which complies with regulations 23(1)(a) and 23(2); and*

(b) *he is satisfied that the requirements of regulation 22(1)(c) (provision of welfare facilities) will be complied with during the construction phase.*

Regulation 17

Regulation

17

The client's duty in relation to the health and safety file

(1) *The client shall ensure that the CDM co-ordinator is provided with all the health and safety information in the client's possession (or which is reasonably obtainable) relating to the project which is likely to be needed for inclusion in the health and safety file, including information specified in regulation 4(9)(c) of the Control of Asbestos Regulations 2006[a].*

(2) *Where a single health and safety file relates to more than one project, site or structure, or where it includes other related information, the client shall ensure that the information relating to each site or structure can be easily identified.*

(3) *The client shall take reasonable steps to ensure that after the construction phase the information in the health and safety file—*

(a) *is kept available for inspection by any person who may need it to comply with the relevant statutory provisions; and*

(b) *is revised as often as may be appropriate to incorporate any relevant new information.*

(4) *It shall be sufficient compliance with paragraph (3)(a) by a client who disposes of his entire interest in the structure if he delivers the health and safety file to the person who acquires his interest in it and ensures that he is aware of the nature and purpose of the file.*

Regulation 18

Regulation

18

Additional duties of designers

(1) *Where a project is notifiable, no designer shall commence work (other than initial design work) in relation to the project unless a CDM co-ordinator has been appointed for the project.*

(2) *The designer shall take all reasonable steps to provide with his design sufficient information about aspects of the design of the structure or its construction or maintenance as will adequately assist the CDM co-ordinator to comply with his duties under these Regulations, including his duties in relation to the health and safety file.*

(a) S.I. 2006/2739.

Regulation 19

Additional duties of contractors

(1)   Where a project is notifiable, no contractor shall carry out construction work in relation to the project unless—

(a)   he has been provided with the names of the CDM co-ordinator and principal contractor;

(b)   he has been given access to such part of the construction phase plan as is relevant to the work to be performed by him, containing sufficient detail in relation to such work; and

(c)   notice of the project has been given to the Executive, or as the case may be the Office of Rail Regulation, under regulation 21.

(2)   Every contractor shall—

(a)   promptly provide the principal contractor with any information (including any relevant part of any risk assessment in his possession or control) which—

(i)   might affect the health or safety of any person carrying out the construction work or of any person who may be affected by it,

(ii)   might justify a review of the construction phase plan, or

(iii)   has been identified for inclusion in the health and safety file in pursuance of regulation 22(1)(j);

(b)   promptly identify any contractor whom he appoints or engages in his turn in connection with the project to the principal contractor;

(c)   comply with—

(i)   any directions of the principal contractor given to him under regulation 22(1)(e), and

(ii)   any site rules;

(d)   promptly provide the principal contractor with the information in relation to any death, injury, condition or dangerous occurrence which the contractor is required to notify or report under the Reporting of Injuries, Diseases and Dangerous Occurrences Regulations 1995[a].

(3)   Every contractor shall—

(a)   in complying with his duty under regulation 13(2) take all reasonable steps to ensure that the construction work is carried out in accordance with the construction phase plan;

(b)   take appropriate action to ensure health and safety where it is not possible to comply with the construction phase plan in any particular case; and

19

(a) S.I. 1995/3163, to which there are amendments not relevant to these Regulations.

Regulation
19

Regulation 20

Regulation

General duties of CDM co-ordinators

(1) The CDM co-ordinator shall—

(a) give suitable and sufficient advice and assistance to the client on undertaking the measures he needs to take to comply with these Regulations during the project (including, in particular, assisting the client in complying with regulations 9 and 16);

(b) ensure that suitable arrangements are made and implemented for the co-ordination of health and safety measures during planning and preparation for the construction phase, including facilitating—

(i) co-operation and co-ordination between persons concerned in the project in pursuance of regulations 5 and 6, and

(ii) the application of the general principles of prevention in pursuance of regulation 7; and

(c) liaise with the principal contractor regarding—

(i) the contents of the health and safety file,

(ii) the information which the principal contractor needs to prepare the construction phase plan, and

(iii) any design development which may affect planning and management of the construction work.

(2) Without prejudice to paragraph (1) the CDM co-ordinator shall—

(a) take all reasonable steps to identify and collect the pre-construction information;

(b) promptly provide in a convenient form to—

(i) every person designing the structure, and

(ii) every contractor who has been or may be appointed by the client (including the principal contractor),

such of the pre-construction information in his possession as is relevant to each;

(c) take all reasonable steps to ensure that designers comply with their duties under regulations 11 and 18(2);

(d) take all reasonable steps to ensure co-operation between designers and the principal contractor during the construction phase in relation to any design or change to a design;

(e) prepare, where none exists, and otherwise review and update a record ("the health and safety file") containing information relating to the project which is likely to be needed during any subsequent construction

20

Regulation 20

work to ensure the health and safety of any person, including the information provided in pursuance of regulations 17(1), 18(2) and 22(1)(j); and

(f) at the end of the construction phase, pass the health and safety file to the client.

Regulation 21

Notification of project by the CDM co-ordinator

Regulation 21

(1) The CDM co-ordinator shall as soon as is practicable after his appointment ensure that notice is given to the Executive containing such of the particulars specified in Schedule 1 as are available.

(2) Where any particulars specified in Schedule 1 have not been notified under paragraph (1) because a principal contractor has not yet been appointed, notice of such particulars shall be given to the Executive as soon as is practicable after the appointment of the principal contractor, and in any event before the start of the construction work.

(3) Any notice under paragraph (1) or (2) shall be signed by or on behalf of the client or, if sent by electronic means, shall otherwise show that he has approved it.

(4) Insofar as the project includes construction work of a description for which the Office of Rail Regulation is made the enforcing authority by regulation 3(1) of the Health and Safety (Enforcing Authority for Railways and Other Guided Transport Systems) Regulations 2006[a], paragraphs (1) and (2) shall have effect as if any reference to the Executive were a reference to the Office of Rail Regulation.

Regulation 22

Duties of the principal contractor

Regulation 22

(1) The principal contractor for a project shall—

(a) plan, manage and monitor the construction phase in a way which ensures that, so far as is reasonably practicable, it is carried out without risks to health or safety, including facilitating—

(i) co-operation and co-ordination between persons concerned in the project in pursuance of regulations 5 and 6, and

(ii) the application of the general principles of prevention in pursuance of regulation 7;

(b) liaise with the CDM co-ordinator in performing his duties in regulation 20(2)(d) during the construction phase in relation to any design or change to a design;

(c) ensure that welfare facilities sufficient to comply with the requirements of Schedule 2 are provided throughout the construction phase;

(a) S.I. 2006/557, to which there are amendments not relevant to these Regulations.

(d) where necessary for health and safety, draw up rules which are appropriate to the construction site and the activities on it (referred to in these Regulations as "site rules");

(e) give reasonable directions to any contractor so far as is necessary to enable the principal contractor to comply with his duties under these Regulations;

(f) ensure that every contractor is informed of the minimum amount of time which will be allowed to him for planning and preparation before he begins construction work;

(g) where necessary, consult a contractor before finalising such part of the construction phase plan as is relevant to the work to be performed by him;

(h) ensure that every contractor is given, before he begins construction work and in sufficient time to enable him to prepare properly for that work, access to such part of the construction phase plan as is relevant to the work to be performed by him;

(i) ensure that every contractor is given, before he begins construction work and in sufficient time to enable him to prepare properly for that work, such further information as he needs—

   (i) to comply punctually with the duty under regulation 13(7), and

   (ii) to carry out the work to be performed by him without risk, so far as is reasonably practicable, to the health and safety of any person;

(j) identify to each contractor the information relating to the contractor's activity which is likely to be required by the CDM co-ordinator for inclusion in the health and safety file in pursuance of regulation 20(2)(e) and ensure that such information is promptly provided to the CDM co-ordinator;

(k) ensure that the particulars required to be in the notice given under regulation 21 are displayed in a readable condition in a position where they can be read by any worker engaged in the construction work; and

(l) take reasonable steps to prevent access by unauthorised persons to the construction site.

(2) The principal contractor shall take all reasonable steps to ensure that every worker carrying out the construction work is provided with—

(a) a suitable site induction;

(b) the information and training referred to in regulation 13(4) by a contractor on whom a duty is placed by that regulation; and

(c) any further information and training which he needs for the particular work to be carried out without undue risk to health or safety.

Regulation 23

Regulation

23

The principal contractor's duty in relation to the construction phase plan

(1)   The principal contractor shall—

(a)   before the start of the construction phase, prepare a construction phase plan which is sufficient to ensure that the construction phase is planned, managed and monitored in a way which enables the construction work to be started so far as is reasonably practicable without risk to health or safety, paying adequate regard to the information provided by the designer under regulations 11(6) and 18(2) and the pre-construction information provided under regulation 20(2)(b);

(b)   from time to time and as often as may be appropriate throughout the project update, review, revise and refine the construction phase plan so that it continues to be sufficient to ensure that the construction phase is planned, managed and monitored in a way which enables the construction work to be carried out so far as is reasonably practicable without risk to health or safety; and

(c)   arrange for the construction phase plan to be implemented in a way which will ensure so far as is reasonably practicable the health and safety of all persons carrying out the construction work and all persons who may be affected by the work.

(2)   The principal contractor shall take all reasonable steps to ensure that the construction phase plan identifies the risks to health and safety arising from the construction work (including the risks specific to the particular type of construction work concerned) and includes suitable and sufficient measures to address such risks, including any site rules.

Regulation 24

Regulation

24

The principal contractor's duty in relation to co-operation and consultation with workers

The principal contractor shall—

(a)   make and maintain arrangements which will enable him and the workers engaged in the construction work to co-operate effectively in promoting and developing measures to ensure the health, safety and welfare of the workers and in checking the effectiveness of such measures;

(b)   consult those workers or their representatives in good time on matters connected with the project which may affect their health, safety or welfare, so far as they or their representatives are not so consulted on those matters by any employer of theirs;

(c)   ensure that such workers or their representatives can inspect and take copies of any information which the principal contractor has, or which these Regulations require to be provided to him, which relates to the planning and management of the project, or which otherwise may affect their health, safety or welfare at the site, except any information—

(i)   the disclosure of which would be against the interests of national security,

(ii)   *which he could not disclose without contravening a prohibition imposed by or under an enactment,*

(iii) *relating specifically to an individual, unless he has consented to its being disclosed,*

(iv)   *the disclosure of which would, for reasons other than its effect on health, safety or welfare at work, cause substantial injury to his undertaking or, where the information was supplied to him by some other person, to the undertaking of that other person, or*

(v)   *obtained by him for the purpose of bringing, prosecuting or defending any legal proceedings.*

PART 4 DUTIES RELATING TO HEALTH AND SAFETY ON CONSTRUCTION SITES

Regulation 25

Application of Regulations 26 to 44

(1) Every contractor carrying out construction work shall comply with the requirements of regulations 26 to 44 insofar as they affect him or any person carrying out construction work under his control or relate to matters within his control.

(2) Every person (other than a contractor carrying out construction work) who controls the way in which any construction work is carried out by a person at work shall comply with the requirements of regulations 26 to 44 insofar as they relate to matters which are within his control.

(3) Every person at work on construction work under the control of another person shall report to that person any defect which he is aware may endanger the health and safety of himself or another person.

(4) Paragraphs (1) and (2) shall not apply to regulation 33, which expressly says on whom the duties in that regulation are imposed.

Regulation
25

Regulation 26

Safe places of work

(1) There shall, so far as is reasonably practicable, be suitable and sufficient safe access to and egress from every place of work and to and from every other place provided for the use of any person while at work, which access and egress shall be properly maintained.

(2) Every place of work shall, so far as is reasonably practicable, be made and kept safe for, and without risks to health to, any person at work there.

(3) Suitable and sufficient steps shall be taken to ensure, so far as is reasonably practicable, that no person uses access or egress, or gains access to any place, which does not comply with the requirements of paragraph (1) or (2) respectively.

(4) Every place of work shall, so far as is reasonably practicable, have sufficient working space and be so arranged that it is suitable for any person who is working or who is likely to work there, taking account of any necessary work equipment present.

Regulation
26

Regulation 27

Good order and site security

(1) Every part of a construction site shall, so far as is reasonably practicable, be kept in good order and every part of a construction site which is used as a place of work shall be kept in a reasonable state of cleanliness.

(2) Where necessary in the interests of health and safety, a construction site shall, so far as is reasonably practicable and in accordance with the level of risk posed, either—

Regulation
27

Regulation
27

(a) have its perimeter identified by suitable signs and be so arranged that its extent is readily identifiable; or

(b) be fenced off,

or both.

(3) No timber or other material with projecting nails (or similar sharp object) shall—

(a) be used in any work; or

(b) be allowed to remain in any place,

if the nails (or similar sharp object) may be a source of danger to any person.

Regulation 28

Stability of structures

Regulation
28

(1) All practicable steps shall be taken, where necessary to prevent danger to any person, to ensure that any new or existing structure or any part of such structure which may become unstable or in a temporary state of weakness or instability due to the carrying out of construction work does not collapse.

(2) Any buttress, temporary support or temporary structure must be of such design and so installed and maintained as to withstand any foreseeable loads which may be imposed on it, and must only be used for the purposes for which it is so designed, installed and maintained.

(3) No part of a structure shall be so loaded as to render it unsafe to any person.

Regulation 29

Demolition or dismantling

Regulation
29

(1) The demolition or dismantling of a structure, or part of a structure, shall be planned and carried out in such a manner as to prevent danger or, where it is not practicable to prevent it, to reduce danger to as low a level as is reasonably practicable.

(2) The arrangements for carrying out such demolition or dismantling shall be recorded in writing before the demolition or dismantling work begins.

Regulation 30

Explosives

Regulation
30

(1) So far as is reasonably practicable, explosives shall be stored, transported and used safely and securely.

(2) Without prejudice to paragraph (1), an explosive charge shall be used or fired only if suitable and sufficient steps have been taken to ensure that no person is exposed to risk of injury from the explosion or from projected or flying material caused thereby.

Regulation 31

Regulation

Excavations

(1)   All practicable steps shall be taken, where necessary to prevent danger to any person, including, where necessary, the provision of supports or battering, to ensure that—

(a)   any excavation or part of an excavation does not collapse;

(b)   no material from a side or roof of, or adjacent to, any excavation is dislodged or falls; and

(c)   no person is buried or trapped in an excavation by material which is dislodged or falls.

(2)   Suitable and sufficient steps shall be taken to prevent any person, work equipment, or any accumulation of material from falling into any excavation

(3)   Without prejudice to paragraphs (1) and (2), suitable and sufficient steps shall be taken, where necessary, to prevent any part of an excavation or ground adjacent to it from being overloaded by work equipment or material;

(4)   Construction work shall not be carried out in an excavation where any supports or battering have been provided pursuant to paragraph (1) unless—

(a)   the excavation and any work equipment and materials which affect its safety, have been inspected by a competent person—

(i)   at the start of the shift in which the work is to be carried out,

(ii)   after any event likely to have affected the strength or stability of the excavation, and

(iii)   after any material unintentionally falls or is dislodged; and

(b)   the person who carried out the inspection is satisfied that the work can be carried out there safely.

(5)   Where the person who carried out the inspection has under regulation 33(1)(a) informed the person on whose behalf the inspection was carried out of any matter about which he is not satisfied, work shall not be carried out in the excavation until the matters have been satisfactorily remedied.

31

Regulation 32

Regulation

Cofferdams and caissons

(1)   Every cofferdam or caisson shall be—

(a)   of suitable design and construction;

(b)   appropriately equipped so that workers can gain shelter or escape if water or materials enter it; and

(c)   properly maintained.

(2)   A cofferdam or caisson shall be used to carry out construction work only if—

32

Regulation 32

(a) the cofferdam or caisson, and any work equipment and materials which affect its safety, have been inspected by a competent person—

    (i) at the start of the shift in which the work is to be carried out, and

    (ii) after any event likely to have affected the strength or stability of the cofferdam or caisson; and

(b) the person who carried out the inspection is satisfied that the work can be safely carried out there.

(3) Where the person who carried out the inspection has under regulation 33(1)(a) informed the person on whose behalf the inspection was carried out of any matter about which he is not satisfied, work shall not be carried out in the cofferdam or caisson until the matters have been satisfactorily remedied.

Regulation 33

Reports of inspections

(1) Subject to paragraph (5), the person who carries out an inspection under regulation 31 or 32 shall, before the end of the shift within which the inspection is completed—

(a) where he is not satisfied that the construction work can be carried out safely at the place inspected, inform the person for whom the inspection was carried out of any matters about which he is not satisfied; and

(b) prepare a report which shall include the particulars set out in Schedule 3.

(2) A person who prepares a report under paragraph (1) shall, within 24 hours of completing the inspection to which the report relates, provide the report or a copy of it to the person on whose behalf the inspection was carried out.

(3) Where the person owing a duty under paragraph (1) or (2) is an employee or works under the control of another, his employer or, as the case may be, the person under whose control he works shall ensure that he performs the duty.

(4) The person on whose behalf the inspection was carried out shall—

(a) keep the report or a copy of it available for inspection by an inspector appointed under section 19 of the Health and Safety at Work etc. Act 1974[a]—

    (i) at the site of the place of work in respect of which the inspection was carried out until that work is completed, and

    (ii) after that for 3 months,

and send to the inspector such extracts from or copies of it as the inspector may from time to time require.

(5) Nothing in this regulation shall require as regards an inspection carried out on a place of work for the purposes of regulations 31(4)(a)(i) and 32(2)(a)(i), the preparation of more than one report within a period of 7 days.

(a) 1974 c.37

Regulation 34

Energy distribution installations

Regulation

(1) Where necessary to prevent danger, energy distribution installations shall be suitably located, checked and clearly indicated.

(2) Where there is a risk from electric power cables—

(a) they shall be directed away from the area of risk; or

(b) the power shall be isolated and, where necessary, earthed; or

(c) if it is not reasonably practicable to comply with paragraph (a) or (b), suitable warning notices and—

    (i) barriers suitable for excluding work equipment which is not needed, or

    (ii) where vehicles need to pass beneath the cables, suspended protections, or

    (iii) in either case, measures providing an equivalent level of safety,

shall be provided or (in the case of measures) taken.

(3) No construction work which is liable to create a risk to health or safety from an underground service, or from damage to or disturbance of it, shall be carried out unless suitable and sufficient steps (including any steps required by this regulation) have been taken to prevent such risk, so far as is reasonably practicable.

34

Regulation 35

Prevention of drowning

Regulation

(1) Where in the course of construction work any person is liable to fall into water or other liquid with a risk of drowning, suitable and sufficient steps shall be taken—

(a) to prevent, so far as is reasonably practicable, such person from so falling;

(b) to minimise the risk of drowning in the event of such a fall; and

(c) to ensure that suitable rescue equipment is provided, maintained and, when necessary, used so that such person may be promptly rescued in the event of such a fall.

(2) Suitable and sufficient steps shall be taken to ensure the safe transport of any person conveyed by water to or from any place of work.

(3) Any vessel used to convey any person by water to or from a place of work shall not be overcrowded or overloaded.

35

Regulation 36

Regulation

Traffic routes

(1) Every construction site shall be organised in such a way that, so far as is reasonably practicable, pedestrians and vehicles can move safely and without risks to health.

(2) Traffic routes shall be suitable for the persons or vehicles using them, sufficient in number, in suitable positions and of sufficient size.

(3) A traffic route shall not satisfy sub-paragraph (2) unless suitable and sufficient steps are taken to ensure that—

(a) pedestrians or vehicles may use it without causing danger to the health or safety of persons near it;

(b) any door or gate for pedestrians which leads onto a traffic route is sufficiently separated from that traffic route to enable pedestrians to see any approaching vehicle or plant from a place of safety;

(c) there is sufficient separation between vehicles and pedestrians to ensure safety or, where this is not reasonably practicable —

(i) there are provided other means for the protection of pedestrians, and

(ii) there are effective arrangements for warning any person liable to be crushed or trapped by any vehicle of its approach;

(d) any loading bay has at least one exit point for the exclusive use of pedestrians; and

(e) where it is unsafe for pedestrians to use a gate intended primarily for vehicles, one or more doors for pedestrians is provided in the immediate vicinity of the gate, is clearly marked and is kept free from obstruction.

(4) Every traffic route shall be—

(a) indicated by suitable signs where necessary for reasons of health or safety;

(b) regularly checked; and

(c) properly maintained.

(5) No vehicle shall be driven on a traffic route unless, so far as is reasonably practicable, that traffic route is free from obstruction and permits sufficient clearance.

36

Regulation 37

Regulation
37

Vehicles

(1) Suitable and sufficient steps shall be taken to prevent or control the unintended movement of any vehicle.

(2)   Suitable and sufficient steps shall be taken to ensure that, where any person may be endangered by the movement of any vehicle, the person having effective control of the vehicle shall give warning to any person who is liable to be at risk from the movement of the vehicle.

(3)   Any vehicle being used for the purposes of construction work shall when being driven, operated or towed—

(a)   be driven, operated or towed in such a manner as is safe in the circumstances; and

(b)   be loaded in such a way that it can be driven, operated or towed safely.

(4)   No person shall ride or be required or permitted to ride on any vehicle being used for the purposes of construction work otherwise than in a safe place thereon provided for that purpose.

(5)   No person shall remain or be required or permitted to remain on any vehicle during the loading or unloading of any loose material unless a safe place of work is provided and maintained for such person.

(6)   Suitable and sufficient measures shall be taken so as to prevent any vehicle from falling into any excavation or pit, or into water, or overrunning the edge of any embankment or earthwork.

Regulation 38

Prevention of risk from fire etc.

Suitable and sufficient steps shall be taken to prevent, so far as is reasonably practicable, the risk of injury to any person during the carrying out of construction work arising from—

(a)   fire or explosion;

(b)   flooding; or

(c)   any substance liable to cause asphyxiation.

Regulation 39

Emergency procedures

(1)   Where necessary in the interests of the health and safety of any person on a construction site, there shall be prepared and, where necessary, implemented suitable and sufficient arrangements for dealing with any foreseeable emergency, which arrangements shall include procedures for any necessary evacuation of the site or any part thereof.

(2)   In making arrangements under paragraph (1), account shall be taken of—

(a)   the type of work for which the construction site is being used;

(b)   the characteristics and size of the construction site and the number and location of places of work on that site;

(c)   the work equipment being used;

(d)   the number of persons likely to be present on the site at any one time; and

(e)   the physical and chemical properties of any substances or materials on or likely to be on the site.

(3)   Where arrangements are prepared pursuant to paragraph (1), suitable and sufficient steps shall be taken to ensure that—

(a)   every person to whom the arrangements extend is familiar with those arrangements; and

(b)   the arrangements are tested by being put into effect at suitable intervals.

Regulation 40

Emergency routes and exits

(1)   Where necessary in the interests of the health and safety of any person on a construction site, a sufficient number of suitable emergency routes and exits shall be provided to enable any person to reach a place of safety quickly in the event of danger.

(2)   An emergency route or exit provided pursuant to paragraph (1) shall lead as directly as possible to an identified safe area.

(3)   Any emergency route or exit provided in accordance with paragraph (1), and any traffic route giving access thereto, shall be kept clear and free from obstruction and, where necessary, provided with emergency lighting so that such emergency route or exit may be used at any time.

(4)   In making provision under paragraph (1), account shall be taken of the matters in regulation 39(2).

(5)   All emergency routes or exits shall be indicated by suitable signs.

Regulation 41

Fire detection and fire-fighting

(1)   Where necessary in the interests of the health and safety of any person at work on a construction site there shall be provided suitable and sufficient—

(a)   fire-fighting equipment; and

(b)   fire detection and alarm systems,

which shall be suitably located.

(2)   In making provision under paragraph (1), account shall be taken of the matters in regulation 39(2).

(3)   Any fire-fighting equipment and any fire detection and alarm system provided under paragraph (1) shall be examined and tested at suitable intervals and properly maintained.

(4)   Any fire-fighting equipment which is not designed to come into use automatically shall be easily accessible.

Regulation

41

(5)   Every person at work on a construction site shall, so far as is reasonably practicable, be instructed in the correct use of any fire-fighting equipment which it may be necessary for him to use.

(6)   Where a work activity may give rise to a particular risk of fire, a person shall not carry out such work unless he is suitably instructed.

(7)   Fire-fighting equipment shall be indicated by suitable signs.

Regulation 42

Fresh air

Regulation

42

(1)   Suitable and sufficient steps shall be taken to ensure, so far as is reasonably practicable, that every place of work or approach thereto has sufficient fresh or purified air to ensure that the place or approach is safe and without risks to health.

(2)   Any plant used for the purpose of complying with paragraph (1) shall, where necessary for reasons of health or safety, include an effective device to give visible or audible warning of any failure of the plant.

Regulation 43

Temperature and weather protection

Regulation

43

(1)   Suitable and sufficient steps shall be taken to ensure, so far as is reasonably practicable, that during working hours the temperature at any place of work indoors is reasonable having regard to the purpose for which that place is used.

(2)   Every place of work outdoors shall, where necessary to ensure the health and safety of persons at work there, be so arranged that, so far as is reasonably practicable and having regard to the purpose for which that place is used and any protective clothing or work equipment provided for the use of any person at work there, it provides protection from adverse weather.

Regulation 44

Lighting

Regulation

44

(1)   Every place of work and approach thereto and every traffic route shall be provided with suitable and sufficient lighting, which shall be, so far as is reasonably practicable, by natural light.

(2)   The colour of any artificial lighting provided shall not adversely affect or change the perception of any sign or signal provided for the purposes of health and safety.

(3)   Without prejudice to paragraph (1), suitable and sufficient secondary lighting shall be provided in any place where there would be a risk to the health or safety of any person in the event of failure of primary artificial lighting.

PART 5 GENERAL

Regulation 45

Civil liability

Breach of a duty imposed by the preceding provisions of these Regulations, other than those imposed by regulations 9(1)(b), 13(6) and (7), 16, 22(1)(c) and (l), 25(1), (2) and (4), 26 to 44 and Schedule 2, shall not confer a right of action in any civil proceedings insofar as that duty applies for the protection of a person who is not an employee of the person on whom the duty is placed.

Regulation 46

Enforcement in respect of fire

(1) Subject to paragraphs (2) and (3)—

(a) in England and Wales the enforcing authority within the meaning of article 25 of the Regulatory Reform (Fire Safety) Order 2005[(a)]; or

(b) in Scotland the enforcing authority within the meaning of section 61 of the Fire (Scotland) Act 2005[(b)],

shall be the enforcing authority in respect of a construction site which is contained within, or forms part of, premises which are occupied by persons other than those carrying out the construction work or any activity arising from such work as regards regulations 39 and 40, in so far as those regulations relate to fire, and regulation 41.

(2) In England and Wales paragraph (1) only applies in respect of premises to which the Regulatory Reform (Fire Safety) Order 2005 applies.

(3) In Scotland paragraph (1) only applies in respect of premises to which Part 3 of the Fire (Scotland) Act 2005 applies[(c)].

Regulation 47

Transitional provisions

(1) These Regulations shall apply in relation to a project which began before their coming into force, with the following modifications.

(2) Subject to paragraph (3), where the time specified in paragraph (1) or (2) of regulation 14 for the appointment of the CDM co-ordinator or the principal contractor occurred before the coming into force of these Regulations, the client shall appoint the CDM co-ordinator or, as the case may be, the principal contractor, as soon as is practicable.

(a) S.I. 2005/1541, to which there are amendments not relevant to these Regulations. All functions of the Secretary of State under the Order, so far as exercisable in relation to Wales, were transferred to the National Assembly for Wales by S.I. 2006/1458.
(b) 2005 asp 5. Section 61(9) was amended by S.I. 2005/2060 article 2(1) and (4)(a) and (b).
(c) Section 77(1) was amended and 77(1A) inserted by S.I. 2005/2060 article 2(1) and (6)(a) and (b); section 77A was inserted by S.I. 2005/2060 article 2(1) and (7); section 78(2) was amended by S.S.I. 2005/352 regulation 2 and S.I. 2005/2060 article 2(1) and (8)(a); section 78(3) was amended and 78(5A) inserted by S.I. 2005/2060 article 2(1) and (8)(b) and (c).

Regulation

(3)   Where a client appoints any planning supervisor or principal contractor already appointed under regulation 6 of the Construction (Design and Management) Regulations 1994[a] (referred to in this regulation as "the 1994 Regulations") as the CDM co-ordinator or the principal contractor respectively pursuant to paragraph (2), regulation 4(1) shall have effect so that the client shall within twelve months of the coming into force of these Regulations take reasonable steps to ensure that any CDM co-ordinator or principal contractor so appointed is competent within the meaning of regulation 4(2).

(4)   Any planning supervisor or principal contractor appointed under regulation 6 of the 1994 Regulations shall, in the absence of an express appointment by the client, be treated for the purposes of paragraph (2) as having been appointed as the CDM co-ordinator, or the principal contractor, respectively.

(5)   Any person treated as having been appointed as the CDM co-ordinator or the principal contractor pursuant to paragraph (4) shall within twelve months of the coming into force of these Regulations take such steps as are necessary to ensure that he is competent within the meaning of regulation 4(2).

(6)   Any agent appointed by a client under regulation 4 of the 1994 Regulations before the coming into force of these Regulations may, if requested by the client and if he himself consents, continue to act as the agent of that client and shall be subject to such requirements and prohibitions as are placed by these Regulations on that client, unless or until such time as such appointment is revoked by that client, or the project comes to an end, or five years elapse from the coming into force of these Regulations, whichever arises first.

(7)   Where notice has been given under regulation 7 of the 1994 Regulations, the references in regulations 19(1)(c) and 22(1)(k) to notice under regulation 21 shall be construed as being to notice under that regulation.

47

Regulation 48

Revocations and amendments

Regulation

(1)   The revocations listed in Schedule 4 shall have effect.

(2)   The amendments listed in Schedule 5 shall have effect.

Signed by authority of the Secretary of State for Work and Pensions.

Bill McKenzie
Parliamentary Under Secretary of State,
7th February 2007   Department for Work and Pensions

(a) S.I. 1994/3140, amended by S.I. 2006/557; there are other amending instruments but none is relevant.

48

Schedule 1

Particulars to be notified to the Executive (or Office of Rail Regulation)

Schedule

Regulation 21(1), (2) and (4)

1   *Date of forwarding.*

2   *Exact address of the construction site.*

3   *The name of the local authority where the site is located.*

4   *A brief description of the project and the construction work which it includes.*

5   *Contact details of the client (name, address, telephone number and any e-mail address).*

6   *Contact details of the CDM co-ordinator (name, address, telephone number and any e-mail address).*

7   *Contact details of the principal contractor (name, address, telephone number and any e-mail address).*

8   *Date planned for the start of the construction phase.*

9   *The time allowed by the client to the principal contractor referred to in regulation 15(b) for planning and preparation for construction work.*

10   *Planned duration of the construction phase.*

11   *Estimated maximum number of people at work on the construction site.*

12   *Planned number of contractors on the construction site.*

13   *Name and address of any contractor already appointed.*

14   *Name and address of any designer already engaged.*

15   *A declaration signed by or on behalf of the client that he is aware of his duties under these Regulations.*

Schedule 2

Welfare facilities

Regulations 9(1)(b), 13(7) and 22(1)(c)

Sanitary conveniences

1   Suitable and sufficient sanitary conveniences shall be provided or made available at readily accessible places. So far as is reasonably practicable, rooms containing sanitary conveniences shall be adequately ventilated and lit.

2   So far as is reasonably practicable, sanitary conveniences and the rooms containing them shall be kept in a clean and orderly condition.

3   Separate rooms containing sanitary conveniences shall be provided for men and women, except where and so far as each convenience is in a separate room, the door of which is capable of being secured from the inside.

Washing facilities

4   Suitable and sufficient washing facilities, including showers if required by the nature of the work or for health reasons, shall so far as is reasonably practicable be provided or made available at readily accessible places.

5   Washing facilities shall be provided—

(a)   in the immediate vicinity of every sanitary convenience, whether or not provided elsewhere; and

(b)   in the vicinity of any changing rooms required by paragraph 14 whether or not provided elsewhere.

6   Washing facilities shall include—

(a)   a supply of clean hot and cold, or warm, water (which shall be running water so far as is reasonably practicable);

(b)   soap or other suitable means of cleaning; and

(c)   towels or other suitable means of drying.

7   Rooms containing washing facilities shall be sufficiently ventilated and lit.

8   Washing facilities and the rooms containing them shall be kept in a clean and orderly condition.

9   Subject to paragraph 10 below, separate washing facilities shall be provided for men and women, except where and so far as they are provided in a room the door of which is capable of being secured from inside and the facilities in each such room are intended to be used by only one person at a time.

10   Paragraph 9 above shall not apply to facilities which are provided for washing hands, forearms and face only.

2

Drinking water

11 An adequate supply of wholesome drinking water shall be provided or made available at readily accessible and suitable places.

12 Every supply of drinking water shall be conspicuously marked by an appropriate sign where necessary for reasons of health and safety.

13 Where a supply of drinking water is provided, there shall also be provided a sufficient number of suitable cups or other drinking vessels unless the supply of drinking water is in a jet from which persons can drink easily.

Changing rooms and lockers

14 (1) Suitable and sufficient changing rooms shall be provided or made available at readily accessible places if—

(a) a worker has to wear special clothing for the purposes of his work; and

(b) he cannot, for reasons of health or propriety, be expected to change elsewhere,

being separate rooms for, or separate use of rooms by, men and women where necessary for reasons of propriety.

(2) Changing rooms shall—

(a) be provided with seating; and

(b) include, where necessary, facilities to enable a person to dry any such special clothing and his own clothing and personal effects.

(3) Suitable and sufficient facilities shall, where necessary, be provided or made available at readily accessible places to enable persons to lock away—

(a) any such special clothing which is not taken home;

(b) their own clothing which is not worn during working hours; and

(c) their personal effects.

Facilities for rest

15 (1) Suitable and sufficient rest rooms or rest areas shall be provided or made available at readily accessible places.

(2) Rest rooms and rest areas shall—

(a) include suitable arrangements to protect non-smokers from discomfort caused by tobacco smoke;

(b) be equipped with an adequate number of tables and adequate seating with backs for the number of persons at work likely to use them at any one time;

(c) where necessary, include suitable facilities for any person at work who is a pregnant woman or nursing mother to rest lying down;

Schedule

2

(d)   *include suitable arrangements to ensure that meals can be prepared and eaten;*

(e)   *include the means for boiling water; and*

(f)   *be maintained at an appropriate temperature.*

Schedule 3

Particulars to be included in a report of inspection

Regulation 33(1)(b)

1   Name and address of the person on whose behalf the inspection was carried out.

2   Location of the place of work inspected.

3   Description of the place of work or part of that place inspected (including any work equipment and materials).

4   Date and time of the inspection.

5   Details of any matter identified that could give rise to a risk to the health or safety of any person.

6   Details of any action taken as a result of any matter identified in paragraph 5 above.

7   Details of any further action considered necessary.

8   Name and position of the person making the report.

Schedule 4

Revocation of instruments

Regulation 48(1)

Description of instrument	Reference	Extent of revocation
The Construction (General Provisions) Regulations 1961	S.I. 1961/1580	The whole Regulations
The Health and Safety Information for Employees Regulations 1989	S.I. 1989/682	Regulation 8(3); part III of the Schedule
The Construction (Design and Management) Regulations 1994	S.I. 1994/3140	The whole Regulations
The Construction (Health, Safety and Welfare) Regulations 1996	S.I. 1996/1592	The whole Regulations
The Health and Safety (Enforcing Authority) Regulations 1998	S.I. 1998/494	In Schedule 3, the entries relating to the Construction (Design and Management) Regulations 1994 and to the Construction (Health, Safety and Welfare) Regulations 1996
The Provision and Use of Work Equipment Regulations 1998	S.I. 1998/2306	In Schedule 4, the entry relating to the Construction (Health, Safety and Welfare) Regulations 1996
The Lifting Operations and Lifting Equipment Regulations 1998	S.I. 1998/2307	In Schedule 2, the entry relating to the Construction (Health, Safety and Welfare) Regulations 1996
The Management of Health and Safety at Work Regulations 1999	S.I. 1999/3242	Regulation 27 In Schedule 2, the entry relating to the Construction (Design and Management) Regulations 1994
The Construction (Design and Management)(Amendment) Regulations 2000	S.I. 2000/2380	The whole Regulations
The Fire and Rescue Services Act 2004 (Consequential Amendments)(England) Order 2004	S.I. 2004/3168	Article 37
The Work at Height Regulations 2005	S.I. 2005/735	In Schedule 8, the entry relating to the Construction (Health, Safety and Welfare) Regulations 1996
The Regulatory Reform (Fire Safety) Order 2005	S.I. 2005/1541	Schedule 3 paragraph 3
The Fire and Rescue Services Act 2004 (Consequential Amendments)(Wales) Order 2005	S.I. 2005/2929	Article 37
The Fire (Scotland) Act 2005 (Consequential Modifications and Amendments)(No.2) Order 2005	S.S.I. 2005/344	Schedule 1 Part 1 paragraph 18
The Fire (Scotland) Act 2005 (Consequential Modifications and Savings)(No.2) Order 2006	S.S.I. 2006/457	Schedule 1 paragraph 4
The Health and Safety (Enforcing Authority for Railways and Other Guided Transport Systems) Regulations 2006	S.I. 2006/557	Schedule paragraph 4

4

Schedule 5

Amendments

Regulation 48(2)

Description of instrument	Reference	Extent of amendment
The Factories Act 1961	1961 c.34, as amended by S.I. 1996/1592	In section 176(1) in the definitions "building operation" and "work of engineering construction" for "1994" substitute "2007"
The Fire (Scotland) Act 2005	2005 asp 5, as amended by S.I. 2005/2060	For the words in section 61(9)(za)(iv) substitute "which are a workplace which is, or is on, a construction site (as defined in regulation 2(1) of the Construction (Design and Management) Regulations 2007) and to which those Regulations apply (other than a construction site to which regulation 46(1) of those Regulations applies)"
The Construction (Head Protection) Regulations 1989	S.I. 1989/2209	For the words in regulation 2(1) substitute "Subject to paragraph (2) of this regulation, these Regulations shall apply to construction work within the meaning of regulation 2(1) of the Construction (Design and Management) Regulations 2007"
The Workplace (Health Safety and Welfare) Regulations 1992	S.I. 1992/3004, as amended by S.I. 1996/1592	For the words in regulation 3(1)(b) substitute "a workplace which is a construction site within the meaning of the Construction (Design and Management) Regulations 2007, and in which the only activity being undertaken is construction work within the meaning of those regulations, save that— (i) regulations 18 and 25A apply to such a workplace; and (ii) regulations 7(1A), 12, 14, 15, 16, 18, 19 and 26(1) apply to such a workplace which is indoors"
The Work in Compressed Air Regulations 1996	S.I. 1996/1656	In regulation 2(1) for the words ""the 1996 Regulations" means the Construction (Health, Safety and Welfare) Regulations 1996" substitute ""the 2007 Regulations" means the Construction (Design and Management) Regulations 2007"
		In regulation 3(1) for "1994" substitute "2007" and for the words "is not excluded by regulation 3(2)" substitute "is carried out in the course of a project which is notifiable within the meaning of regulation 2(3)"
		In regulation 5(3) for "1994" substitute "2007"
		In regulation 13(2)(a) for the words "19, 20 and 25(3) of the 1996 Regulations" substitute "39, 40 and 44(3) of the 2007 Regulations"
		In regulation 13(2)(d) for the words "20(1) of the 1996 Regulations" substitute "39(1) of the 2007 Regulations"
		In regulation 14(1) for the words "21 of the 1996 Regulations" substitute "41 of the 2007 Regulations"

5

In regulation 18(a) for the words "regulation 22 of the 1996 Regulations" substitute "Schedule 2 of the 2007 Regulations"

The Railway Safety (Miscellaneous Provisions) Regulations 1997	S.I. 1997/553	In regulation 2(1) in the definition "construction work" for "1994" substitute "2007"
The Fire Precautions (Workplace) Regulations 1997	S.I. 1997/1840	In regulation 3(5)(d) for the words "the Construction (Health, Safety and Welfare) Regulations 1996" substitute "the Construction (Design and Management) Regulations 2007"
The Health and Safety (Enforcing Authority) Regulations 1998	S.I. 1998/494	In regulation 2(1) in the definitions "construction work" and "contractor" for "1994" substitute "2007" In Schedule 2 for the words in paragraph 4(a)(i) substitute "the project which includes the work is notifiable within the meaning of regulation 2(3) of the Construction (Design and Management) Regulations 2007; or"
The Provision and Use of Work Equipment Regulations 1998	S.I. 1998/2306	In regulation 6(5)(e) for the words "regulation 29 of the Construction (Health, Safety and Welfare) Regulations 1996" substitute "regulations 31(4) or 32(2) of the Construction (Design and Management) Regulations 2007"
The Gas Safety (Installation and Use) Regulations 1998	S.I. 1998/2451	In regulation 2(4)(d) for "1994" substitute "2007"
The Work at Height Regulations 2005	S.I. 2005/735	In regulation 2(1) in the definition "construction work" for the words "the Construction (Health, Safety and Welfare) Regulations 1996" substitute "the Construction (Design and Management) Regulations 2007"
The Regulatory Reform (Fire Safety) Order 2005	S.I. 2005/1541	In article 25(b)(iv) for the words "the Construction (Health, Safety and Welfare) Regulations 1996" substitute "the Construction (Design and Management) Regulations 2007" and for "33" substitute "46"
The Health and Safety (Enforcing Authority for Railways and Other Guided Transport Systems) Regulations 2006	S.I. 2006/557	In regulation 2 in the definition "construction work" for "1994" substitute "2007" For the words in regulation 5(2)(a)(i) substitute "the project which includes that work is notifiable within the meaning of regulation 2(3) of the Construction (Design and Management) Regulations 2007; and"

Appendix 2

Pre-construction information

When drawing up the pre-construction information, each of the following topics should be considered. Information should be included where the topic is relevant to the work proposed. The pre-construction information provides information for those bidding for or planning work, and for the development of the construction phase plan. **The level of detail in the information should be proportionate to the risks involved in the project.**

Pre-construction information

1 Description of project

(a) project description and programme details including:

   (i) key dates (including planned start and finish of the construction phase), and

   (ii) the minimum time to be allowed between appointment of the principal contractor and instruction to commence work on site;

(b) details of client, designers, CDM co-ordinator and other consultants;

(c) whether or not the structure will be used as a workplace (in which case, the finished design will need to take account of the relevant requirements of the Workplace (Health, Safety and Welfare) Regulations 1992);

(d) extent and location of existing records and plans.

2 Client's considerations and management requirements

(a) arrangements for:

   (i) planning for and managing the construction work, including any health and safety goals for the project,

   (ii) communication and liaison between client and others,

   (iii) security of the site,

   (iv) welfare provision;

(b) requirements relating to the health and safety of the client's employees or customers or those involved in the project such as:

   (i) site hoarding requirements,

   (ii) site transport arrangements or vehicle movement restrictions,

   (iii) client permit-to-work systems,

   (iv) fire precautions,

   (v) emergency procedures and means of escape,

   (vi) 'no-go' areas or other authorisation requirements for those involved in the project,

(vii) any areas the client has designated as confined spaces,

(viii) smoking and parking restrictions.

3   *Environmental restrictions and existing on-site risks*

(a)   Safety hazards, including:

     (i)   boundaries and access, including temporary access – for example narrow streets, lack of parking, turning or storage space,

     (ii)   any restrictions on deliveries or waste collection or storage,

     (iii)   adjacent land uses – for example schools, railway lines or busy roads,

     (iv)   existing storage of hazardous materials,

     (v)   location of existing services particularly those that are concealed – water, electricity, gas, etc,

     (vi)   ground conditions, underground structures or water courses where this might affect the safe use of plant, for example cranes, or the safety of groundworks,

     (vii) information about existing structures – stability, structural form, fragile or hazardous materials, anchorage points for fall arrest systems (particularly where demolition is involved),

     (viii) previous structural modifications, including weakening or strengthening of the structure (particularly where demolition is involved),

     (ix)   fire damage, ground shrinkage, movement or poor maintenance which may have adversely affected the structure,

     (x)   any difficulties relating to plant and equipment in the premises, such as overhead gantries whose height restricts access,

     (xi)   health and safety information contained in earlier design, construction or 'as-built' drawings, such as details of pre-stressed or post-tensioned structures;

(b)   health hazards, including:

     (i)   asbestos, including results of surveys (particularly where demolition is involved),

     (ii)   existing storage of hazardous materials,

     (iii)   contaminated land, including results of surveys,

     (iv)   existing structures containing hazardous materials,

     (v)   health risks arising from client's activities.

4 Significant design and construction hazards

(a) significant design assumptions and suggested work methods, sequences or other control measures;

(b) arrangements for co-ordination of ongoing design work and handling design changes;

(c) information on significant risks identified during design;

(d) materials requiring particular precautions.

5 The health and safety file

Description of its format and any conditions relating to its content.

Appendix 3

Construction phase plan

When drawing up the construction phase plan, you should consider each of the following topics. Information should be included in the plan where the topic is relevant to the work proposed. The plan sets out how health and safety is to be managed during the construction phase. **The level of detail should be proportionate to the risks involved in the project.**

Construction phase plan

1 Description of project

(a) project description and programme details including any key dates;

(b) details of client, CDM co-ordinator, designers, principal contractor and other consultants;

(c) extent and location of existing records and plans that are relevant to health and safety on site, including information about existing structures when appropriate.

2 Management of the work

(a) management structure and responsibilities;

(b) health and safety goals for the project and arrangements for monitoring and review of health and safety performance;

(c) arrangements for:

(i) regular liaison between parties on site,

(ii) consultation with the workforce,

(iii) the exchange of design information between the client, designers, CDM co-ordinator and contractors on site,

(iv) handling design changes during the project,

(v) the selection and control of contractors,

(vi) the exchange of health and safety information between contractors,

(vii) site security,

(viii) site induction,

(ix) on site training,

(x) welfare facilities and first aid,

(xi) the reporting and investigation of accidents and incidents including near misses,

(xii) the production and approval of risk assessments and written systems of work;

(d) site rules (including drug and alcohol policy);

(e) fire and emergency procedures.

3   Arrangements for controlling significant site risks

(a) Safety risks, including:

(i) delivery and removal of materials (including waste*) and work equipment taking account of any risks to the public, for example during access to or egress from the site,

(ii) dealing with services - water, electricity and gas, including overhead powerlines and temporary electrical installations,

(iii) accommodating adjacent land use,

(iv) stability of structures whilst carrying out construction work, including temporary structures and existing unstable structures,

(v) preventing falls,

(vi) work with or near fragile materials,

(vii) control of lifting operations,

(viii) the maintenance of plant and equipment,

(ix) work on excavations and work where there are poor ground conditions,

(x) work on wells, underground earthworks and tunnels,

(xi) work on or near water where there is a risk of drowning,

(xii) work involving diving,

(xiii) work in a caisson or compressed air working,

(xiv) work involving explosives,

(xv) traffic routes and segregation of vehicles and pedestrians,

(xvi) storage of materials (particularly hazardous materials) and work equipment,

(xvii) any other significant safety risks;

* Regulations made under the Clean Neighbourhoods and Environment Act 2005 are expected to require that from October 2007 all construction projects above a given value will be required to write and implement a site waste management plan (SWMP). The SWMP will record the amount of each type of waste that is expected to arise on site and whether it can be reused, recycled or needs to be disposed of. During construction the plan will be updated to map what happens against what was expected to happen, allowing lessons to be learned for future projects. Non-statutory guidance will explain the SWMP process in further detail.

(b) health risks, including:

    (i) the removal of asbestos,

    (ii) dealing with contaminated land,

    (iii) manual handling,

    (iv) use of hazardous substances, particularly where there is a need for health monitoring,

    (v) reducing noise and vibration,

    (vi) work with ionising radiation,

    (vii) exposure to UV radiation (from the sun),

    (viii) any other significant health risks.

4 The health and safety file

(a) layout and format;

(b) arrangements for the collection and gathering of information;

(c) storage of information.

Appendix 4

Competence

Core criteria for demonstration of competence:

Companies, contractors, CDM co-ordinators and designers

You need to meet the standards set out in the core criteria table on pages 110-113. **Column 1** of the table lists the elements which should be assessed when establishing whether or not a company is competent for the work which it will be expected to do. **Column 2** lists the standards against which the assessment should be made. **Column 3** gives some examples of how a company might demonstrate that it meets these standards.

Companies do not have to produce all of the evidence listed in Column 3 to satisfy the standard - they simply need to produce enough evidence to show that they meet the standard in Column 2, taking account of the nature of the project and the risks which the work entails. This requires you to make a judgement as to whether the evidence provided meets the standard to be achieved. **If your judgement is reasonable, and clearly based on the evidence you have asked for and been provided with, you will not be criticised if the company you appoint subsequently proves not to be competent when carrying out the work.**

Remember that assessments should focus on the needs of the particular job and should be proportionate to the risks arising from the work. Unnecessary bureaucracy associated with competency assessment obscures the real issues and diverts effort away from them.

If you employ less than five persons you do not have to write down your policy, organisation or arrangements under criteria 1 and 2. However, you do need to demonstrate that your policy and arrangements are adequate in relation to the type of work you do. Assessments of competence will be made easier if your procedures are clear and accessible.

'Contractor', 'Designer' and 'CDM co-ordinator' relate to your function, not to the type of organisation.

	Criteria	Standard to be achieved	Examples of the evidence that you could use to demonstrate you meet the required standard
	Stage 1 assessment		
1	Health and safety policy and organisation for health and safety	You are expected to have and implement an appropriate policy, regularly reviewed, and signed off by the Managing Director or equivalent. The policy must be relevant to the nature and scale of your work and set out the responsibilities for health and safety management at all levels within the organisation.	A signed, current copy of the company policy (indicating when it was last reviewed and by whose authority it is published). Guidance on writing company policies for health and safety can be found in HSE free leaflet INDG259.[7]
2	Arrangements	These should set out the arrangements for health and safety management within the organisation and should be relevant to the nature and scale of your work. They should set out how the company will discharge their duties under CDM2007. There should be a clear indication of how these arrangements are communicated to the workforce.	A clear explanation of the arrangements which the company has made for putting its policy into effect and for discharging its duties under CDM2007. Guidance on making arrangements for the management of health and safety can be found in HSE free leaflet INDG259.[7]
3	Competent advice – corporate and construction-related	Your organisation, and your employees, must have ready access to competent health and safety advice, preferably from within your own organisation. The advisor must be able to provide general health and safety advice, and also (from the same source or elsewhere) advice relating to construction health and safety issues.	Name and competency details of the source of advice, for example a safety group, trade federation, or consultant who provides health and safety information and advice. An example from the last 12 months of advice given and action taken.
4	Training and information	You should have in place, and implement, training arrangements to ensure your employees have the skills and understanding necessary to discharge their duties as contractors, designers or CDM co-ordinators. You should have in place a programme for refresher training, for example a Continuing Professional Development (CPD) programme or life-long learning which will keep your employees updated on new developments and changes to legislation or good health and safety practice. This applies throughout the organisation - from Board or equivalent, to trainees.	Headline training records. Evidence of a health and safety training culture including records, certificates of attendance and adequate health and safety induction training for site-based workforce. Evidence of an active CPD programme. Sample 'toolbox talks'.
5	Individual qualifications and experience	Employees are expected to have the appropriate qualifications and experience for the assigned tasks, unless they are under controlled and competent supervision.	Details of qualifications and/or experience of specific corporate post holders for example Board members, health and safety advisor etc. Other key roles should be named or identified and details of relevant qualifications and experience provided. **For contractors:** details of number/percentage of people engaged in the project who have passed a construction health and safety assessment, for example the CITB Construction Skills touch screen test or similar schemes, such as the CCNSG equivalent.

	Criteria	Standard to be achieved	Examples of the evidence that you could use to demonstrate you meet the required standard
			For site managers, details of any specific training such as the Construction Skills CITB 'Site Management Safety Training Scheme' certificate or equivalent. For professionals, details of qualifications and/or professional institution membership. For site workers, details of any relevant qualifications or training such as S/NVQ certificates. Evidence of a company-based training programme suitable for the work to be carried out. **For design organisations** - details of number/percentage of people engaged in the project who have passed a construction health and safety assessment, for example the CITB Construction Skills touch screen test or affiliated schemes, or the CCNSG equivalent. Details of any relevant qualifications and/or professional institution membership and any other specific qualifications such as ICE construction health and safety register, NEBOSH Construction Certificate, APS Design Register. **For CDM co-ordinators** - details of number/percentage of people engaged in the project who have passed a construction health and safety assessment, for example the CITB Construction Skills touch screen test or affiliated schemes, or the CCNSG equivalent. Evidence of health and safety knowledge such as NEBOSH Construction Certificate. Details of professional institution membership and any other specific qualifications such as member of the CDM co-ordinators' register administered by the APS or ICS (formerly the IPS), or the ICE construction health and safety register etc. Evidence of a clear commitment to training and the Continuing Professional Development of staff.
6	Monitoring, audit and review	You should have a system for monitoring your procedures, for auditing them at periodic intervals, and for reviewing them on an ongoing basis.	Could be through formal audit or discussions/reports to senior managers. Evidence of recent monitoring and management response. Copies of site inspection reports.
7	Workforce involvement	You should have, and implement, an established means of consulting with your workforce on health and safety matters.	Evidence showing how consultation is carried out. Records of health and safety committees. Names of appointed safety representatives (trade union or other). For those employing less than five, be able to describe how you consult with your employees to achieve the consultation required.

	Criteria	Standard to be achieved	Examples of the evidence that you could use to demonstrate you meet the required standard
8	Accident reporting and enforcement action; follow-up investigation	You should have records of all RIDDOR (the Reporting of Injuries, Diseases and Dangerous Occurrences Regulations 1999)[8] reportable events for at least the last three years. You should also have in place a system for reviewing all incidents, and recording the action taken as a result. You should record any enforcement action taken against your company over the last five years, and the action which you have taken to remedy matters subject to enforcement action.	Evidence showing the way in which you record and investigate accidents and incidents. Records of last two accidents/incidents and action taken to prevent recurrence. Records of any enforcement action taken over the last five years, and what action was taken to put matters right (information on enforcement taken by HSE over the last five years is available on the HSE website). For larger companies, simple statistics showing incidence rates of major injuries, over three-day injuries, reportable cases of ill health and dangerous occurrences for the last three years. Records should include any incidents that occurred whilst the company traded under a different name, and any incidents that occur to direct employees or labour-only sub-contractors.
9	Sub-contracting/consulting procedures (if applicable)	You should have arrangements in place for appointing competent sub-contractors/consultants. You should be able to demonstrate how you ensure that sub-contractors will also have arrangements for appointing competent sub-contractors or consultants. You should have arrangements for monitoring sub-contractor performance.	Evidence showing how you ensure sub-contractors are competent. Examples of sub-contractor assessments you have carried out. Evidence showing how you require similar standards of competence assessment from sub-contractors. Evidence showing how you monitor sub-contractor performance.
10	Hazard elimination and risk control (designers only)	You should have, and implement, arrangements for meeting your duties under regulation 11 of CDM2007.	Evidence showing how you: ensure co-operation and co-ordination of design work within the design team and with other designers/contractors; ensure that hazards are eliminated and any remaining risks controlled; ensure that any structure which will be used as a workplace will meet relevant requirements of the Workplace (Health, Safety and Welfare) Regulations 1992. Examples showing how risk was reduced through design. A short summary of how changes to designs will be managed. (Note: the emphasis here should be on practical measures which reduce particular risks arising from the design, not on lengthy procedural documentation highlighting generic risks.)

	Criteria	Standard to be achieved	Examples of the evidence that you could use to demonstrate you meet the required standard
11	Risk assessment leading to a safe method of work (**contractors only**)	You should have procedures in place for carrying out risk assessments and for developing and implementing safe systems of work/method statements.	Evidence showing how the company will identify significant health and safety risks and how they will be controlled. Sample risk assessments/safe systems of work/method statements. If you employ less than five persons and do not have written arrangements, you should be able to describe how you achieve the above.
		The identification of health issues is expected to feature prominently in this system.	This will depend upon the nature of the work, but must reflect the importance of this risk area.
12	Co-operating with others and co-ordinating your work with that of other contractors (**contractors**)	You should be able to illustrate how co-operation and co-ordination of your work is achieved in practice, and how you involve the workforce in drawing up method statements/safe systems of work.	Evidence could include sample risk assessments, procedural arrangements, project team meeting notes. Evidence of how the company co-ordinates its work with other trades.
13	Welfare provisionn (**contractors**)	You should be able to demonstrate how you will ensure that appropriate welfare facilities will be in place before people start work on site.	Evidence could include for example health and safety policy commitment; contracts with welfare facility providers; details of type of welfare facilities provided on previous projects.
14	CDM co-ordinator's duties (**CDM co-ordinators**)	You should be able to demonstrate how you go about encouraging co-operation, co-ordination and communication between designers.	The evidence should be in the form of actual examples rather than by generic procedures.
	Stage 2 assessment		
1	Work experience	You should give details of relevant experience in the field of work for which you are applying.	A simple record of recent projects/contracts should be kept, with the phone numbers/addresses of contacts who can verify that work was carried out with due regard to health and safety. This should be sufficient to demonstrate your ability to deal with the key health and safety issues arising from the work you are applying for. Where there are significant shortfalls in your previous experience, or there are risks associated with the project which you have not managed before, an explanation of how these shortcomings will be overcome.

Appendix 5

Guidance for assessing competence of a CDM co-ordinator for a larger or more complex project, or one with high or unusual risks

Organisations do not have to produce all of the evidence listed in column 3 to **satisfy the standard** - they simply need to produce enough evidence to show that they meet the standard in column 2, taking account of the nature of the project and the risks which the work entails. This requires you to make a judgement as to whether the evidence provided meets the standard to be achieved. **If your judgement is reasonable, and clearly based on the evidence provided, you will not be criticised if the company you appoint subsequently proves not to be competent to carry out the work.**

Remember that assessments should focus on the needs of the particular job and should be proportionate to the risks arising from the work. **Unnecessary bureaucracy associated with competency assessment obscures the real issues and diverts effort away from them.**

Stage	Knowledge and experience standard	Field of knowledge and experience	Examples of attainment which should indicate competence
Stage 1	Task knowledge appropriate for the tasks to be undertaken. May be technical or managerial.	The design and construction process.	Professionally Qualified to Chartered level (Note 1). Membership of a relevant construction institution, for example CIBSE; ICE; IEE; IMechE; IStructE; RIBA; CIAT; CIOB.
	Health and safety knowledge sufficient to perform the task safely, by identifying hazard and evaluating the risk in order to protect self and others, and to appreciate general background.	Health and safety in construction.	Validated CPD in this field, and typical additional qualification for example: NEBOSH Construction Certificate; Member of health and safety register administered by the ICE (Note 2); Membership of Association for Project Safety; Membership of Institution of Construction Safety (formerly the Institution of Planning Supervisors).
Stage 2	Experience and ability sufficient to perform the task, (including where appropriate an appreciation of constructability), to recognise personal limitations, task-related faults and errors and to identify appropriate actions.	Experience relevant to the task.	Evidence of significant work on similar projects with comparable hazards, complexity and procurement route.

Notes
1   Chartered membership of a recognised construction-related institution.
2   Open to any member of a construction-related institution.

Appendix 6

Development of competence: Timeline for an unskilled construction worker

(Not an apprentice or trainee on a recognised training programme)

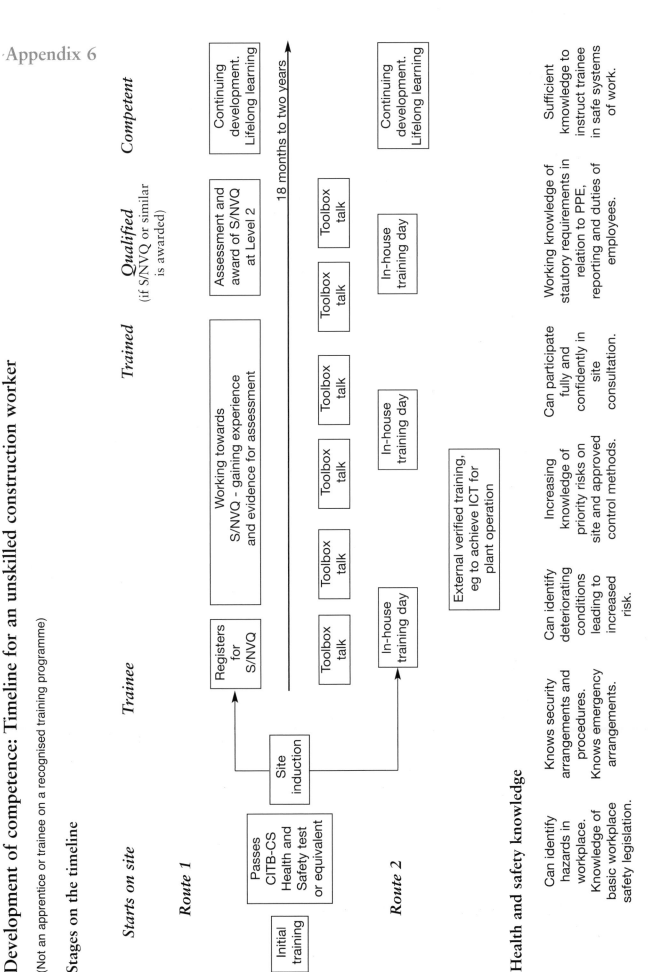

Appendix 7

The principles of prevention

Dutyholders should use these principles to direct their approach to identifying and implementing precautions which are necessary to control risks associated with a project.

The general principles of prevention

(a)   avoiding risks;

(b)   evaluating the risks which cannot be avoided;

(c)   combating the risks at source;

(d)   adapting the work to the individual, especially as regards the design of workplaces, the choice of work equipment and the choice of working and production methods, with a view, in particular, to alleviating monotonous work and work at a predetermined work-rate and to reducing their effect on health;

(e)   adapting to technical progress;

(f)   replacing the dangerous by the non-dangerous or the less dangerous;

(g)   developing a coherent overall prevention policy which covers technology, organisation of work, working conditions, social relationships and the influence of factors relating to the working environment;

(h)   giving collective protective measures priority over individual protective measures; and

(i)   giving appropriate instructions to employees.

References

1 *Management of health and safety at work. Management of Health and Safety at Work Regulations 1999. Approved Code of Practice and guidance* L21 (Second edition) HSE Books 2000 ISBN 0 7176 2488 9

2 *Work with materials containing asbestos. Control of Asbestos Regulations 2006. Approved Code of Practice and guidance* L143 HSE Books 2006 ISBN 0 7176 6206 3

3 *Workplace health, safety and welfare. Workplace (Health, Safety and Welfare) Regulations 1992. Approved Code of Practice* L24 HSE Books 1992 ISBN 0 7176 0413 6

4 *The Building Regulations 2000* SI 2000/2531 The Stationery Office 2000 ISBN 0 11 099 897 9

5 *Safety representatives and safety committees* L87 (Third edition) HSE Books 1996 ISBN 0 7176 1220 1

6 *A guide to the Health and Safety (Consultation with Employees) Regulations 1996. Guidance on Regulations* L95 HSE Books 1996 ISBN 0 7176 1234 1

7 *An introduction to health and safety: Health and safety in small businesses* Leaflet INDG259(rev1) HSE Books 2003 (single copy free) Web version: www.hse.gov.uk/pubns/indg259.pdf

8 *A guide to the Reporting of Injuries, Diseases and Dangerous Occurrences Regulations 1995* L73 (Second edition) HSE Books 1999 ISBN 0 7176 2431 5

HSE priced and free publications are available by mail order from HSE Books, PO Box 1999, Sudbury, Suffolk CO10 2WA Tel: 01787 881165 Fax: 01787 313995 Website: www.hsebooks.co.uk (HSE priced publications are also available from bookshops and free leaflets can be downloaded from HSE's website: www.hse.gov.uk.)

For information about health and safety ring HSE's Infoline Tel: 0845 345 0055 Fax: 0845 408 9566 Textphone: 0845 408 9577 e-mail: hse.infoline@natbrit.com or write to HSE Information Services, Caerphilly Business Park, Caerphilly CF83 3GG.

Printed and published by the Health and Safety Executive   C250   02/07